GW00600853

CONTENTS

DON'T HANG AROUND
We'll help you with your tax

If you get a tax return this April, don't put it away and forget about it. There are lots of good reasons why you should start filling it in straight away:

You may be due a tax rebate. The sooner you post off your tax return, the quicker you will find out.

If you usually get a tax bill, getting your tax return in fast will give you the longest possible notice of next January's payment. Or if you're an employee it means any tax due under £1000 can usually be collected through your PAYE coding.

Also, the earlier you contact us the easier it will be to get advice.

If you need help, contact your tax office during office hours (the telephone number is at the top of your tax return). Or in the evening and at weekends, call the Self Assessment Helpline on 0645 000 444 (calls are charged at local rates).

Self Assessment- a clearer tax syst

DATES TO REMEMBER

When	Who	What
From April 1996	Everyone	Started keeping records of their tax affairs
By 31 January 1997	People who pay tax 'on account' – mainly the self-employed	Had to make their first payment on their 1996/1997 tax bill
6 April 1997	Everyone who receives a Tax Return	Will be sent the new self-assessment Return for 1996/1997 tax year
By 31 May 1997	Employees	Given their P60 for the 1996/1997 tax year by their employer detailing their salary, Income Tax and National Insurance
By 6 July 1997	Employees with expenses and other taxable benefits such as company cars	Will get details of these from their employer for the 1996/1997 tax year – on the form P11D
By 31 July 1997	People paying tax 'on account' – mainly the self-employed	Should pay their second tax instalment for the 1996/1997 tax year. You will receive a demand if this affects you
By 30 September 1997	People who *do not* want to calculate their own tax bill PAYE employees who want the tax they owe collected through their PAYE code (up to £1000)	Should send back their completed Tax Return
5 October 1997	People with new sources of income	Should inform the Inland Revenue
By 31 January 1998	Everyone who receives a Tax Return Partnerships People liable for Capital Gains Tax	Should send it back by now and pay any tax due Should file their Tax Returns and pay any tax due Should pay the CGT tax bill
On 1 February 1998	Anyone who had not sent their tax return back by yesterday's deadline	Gets fined £1009
28 February 1998	Anyone still owing tax due on 31 January 1998	Suffers a 5% surcharge on the tax they owe
Before 31 January 1999	Everyone can still hear from the Inland Revenue about their 1996/1997 Tax Return	Because if the Inland Revenue has any queries they will contact you within 12 months

Tax is a very technical and complex subject and some tax rules are open to interpretation. That is why there is a whole army of accountants employed to make the most of the rules and challenge them. Every effort has been made to ensure the accuracy of this book. Technical tax points have been checked with the Inland Revenue and several qualified accountants. However, as tax rules can be implemented differently and the advice you receive can vary from Tax Office to Tax Office, if you are unsure about any point ask your tax inspector. The number of your Tax Office is written on the top of your Tax Return.

The Institute of Chartered Accountants in England and Wales
The Institute of Chartered Accountants in England and Wales is endorsing the publication of *Self Assessment: How to Fill in your Tax Return*. It has not been responsible for compiling the editorial contents, any queries concerning which should be directed to Kogan Page.

For further information and advice in finding a chartered accountant to help you with Self Assessment, please call the Institute on 0171 920 8633.

Tax Forms are printed with the permission of the Inland Revenue.

Cartoons by McTrusty.

WHY YOU SHOULD READ THIS BOOK

THE TAX SYSTEM IS CHANGING AND YOU NEED TO KNOW HOW THIS WILL AFFECT YOU

Self Assessment is the biggest change to the administration of taxation for 50 years and you must be ready for it. It will affect **8.5 million taxpayers** – the one in three who are sent a Tax Return (the document asking for details of your income and profits) – and means that **you have to take more responsibility for your tax affairs**. New Tax Returns were sent out in April 1997 and need to be completed by 31 January 1998, so it is important to learn how you are going to be affected **now**.

THIS BOOK SHOULD HELP TO TAKE THE FEAR OUT OF TAX

This book translates tax terms into plain English, gives you a basic course in how the tax system works and includes a step-by-step guide to filling in your Tax Return. Once you cut through the terminology you will find tax much easier to understand and be able to fill in your Tax Return with a little less trepidation.

THIS BOOK COULD HELP YOU TO SAVE MONEY

This book tells you: how to fill in your Tax Return yourself so you can save on accountancy fees; how to meet the deadlines to avoid the £100 minimum fine; and how to save on tax. **Self Assessment could mean that taxpayers waste £1.4 billion in tax – over £150 each – by missing deadlines and failing to make the most of the changes to the tax system.**

In this book tax terminology is kept to a minimum and, where it is used, is explained in easy-to-understand terms.

SELF ASSESSMENT OF TAX

Self Assessment is a new way of administering tax. It is **not** a new tax.

WHAT DOES SELF ASSESSMENT MEAN?

You can calculate your own tax if you want to

In theory Self Assessment means you must assess your own tax bill. However, you may be relieved to know that in practice you **do not** actually have to do the calculations yourself, although you can if you want to. The Inland Revenue will calculate your tax bill, but only if you send in your completed Tax Return by **30 September 1997**.

You will get a new style Tax Return

The new Tax Return covers income and capital gains. In the past you may have received more than one Tax Return; in future you will receive one set of documents covering all income and gains.

You will have fixed dates for paying tax

Self Assessment will introduce two tax payment dates – 31 January and 31 July – replacing a confusing series of deadlines which depended on the type of income. More than half of all taxpayers will only have to pay **one bill** a year. If you are self-employed, in partnership, earn income from land and property or large amounts of untaxed investment income you may have **three** bills to pay each year –

two tax instalments or payments *on account* on 31 January and 31 July and a final settling payment on 31 January the year after. Some 1.6 million taxpayers had to make these payments on 31 January 1997.

If you owe a small amount of tax (less than £1000) and are an employee paid under PAYE (the Pay-As-You-Earn tax system), you may not get a tax bill at all provided you send in your Tax Return by 30 September 1997. The extra tax can be collected with the rest of your Income Tax from your salary.

You get one point of contact for all your tax enquiries

Instead of having to deal with different tax offices for different types of tax, you will deal with only one tax office in future. If you are self-employed this will usually be the tax office covering your business address. If you are an employee, this will usually be your existing employer's tax office.

All income will now be taxed on a current year basis

This will particularly affect the **self-employed** and those in **partnership** if they started in business before 6 April 1994 and those who receive **income from abroad** and **interest paid gross** if they started to receive this income before 6 April 1994.

In the past some income was taxed on a *preceding year basis*, meaning there was a time lag between earning money and paying tax on it. It meant that income earned in 1995 did not have to be included on your Tax Return until 1997. This year that changes.

The taxpayers mentioned above may have to provide details of two years of income – the *preceding year* 1995 to 1996 and the *current year* 1996 to 1997. But **they will only pay half the tax owed for both years**.

WHAT YOU MUST DO UNDER SELF ASSESSMENT

You must keep records

You may have already been alerted to the fact that since April 1996 you should have been keeping records of all financial documents. If you have not been keeping records, start *now*.

You must keep your documents for at least 22 months after the end of the tax year to which they relate. So for the April 1996 to April 1997 tax year you must keep records until February 1999. However, if you are self-employed or a partner you must keep your tax records for **five years** after the date you send back your Tax Return. The types of records you need to keep are listed at the beginning of each chapter.

Record keeping means looking after all documents from the Inland Revenue, your bank or building society and your employer, and keeping any paperwork relating to investments, the purchase or sale of assets (such as shares, land, business and investments), as well as detailed accounts of any income and expenditure if you are self-employed. You must set up a record-keeping system, keep documents safe and for as long as required and update your records regularly.

If you fail to keep adequate records to back up your Tax Return the Inland Revenue may fine you up to £3000. Even if you do not get fined, failure to keep records will have other implications – you will find it much harder to fill in your Tax Return.

You must let the Inland Revenue know if your circumstances change

If you start to receive additional untaxed income (income from which tax has not already been deducted) you must tell your tax office within **six months** of the end of the tax year. So for the tax year ending 5 April 1997, the deadline is 5 October 1997. If you do not, the Inland Revenue cannot send you the necessary extra pages that make up your Tax Return.

You must complete and send back your Tax Return on time

You have to fill in your Tax Return for the April 1996 to April 1997 tax year by one of two dates:

❏ **30 September 1997:** if you want the Inland Revenue to calculate how much tax you owe
or if you owe less than £1000 in tax and want that tax collected through your pay packet under the PAYE (Pay-As-You-Earn) tax system instead of paying a tax bill.

❏ **31 January 1998:** for all other Tax Returns.

You must send your Tax Return in a few days earlier to make sure that it reaches the Inland Revenue *by* the deadline. If you miss the '30 September deadline, the Inland Revenue will still work out your tax bill but cannot guarantee that it will let you know how much tax you must pay before the 31 January 1998 payment deadline. As a result you may have to pay interest on outstanding tax.

Fixed penalties
Fixed penalties for Tax Returns not sent back by 31 January are **£100**. If your Return is still outstanding six months later you will pay a further **£100**. However, if you do not owe £100 or more in tax, the penalty will be reduced to the amount of tax owed. These fixed fines are charged automatically. If you are very tardy the fines get heftier. If the Inland Revenue thinks that charging you the fixed penalty is not going to make you send back your Tax Return, fines of up to **£60 a day** can be levied.

If you do not send back your Tax Return and do not pay your tax by the 31 January 1998 deadline, the Inland Revenue may bill you for the tax it thinks you owe, plus penalties and surcharges, and collect that amount.

In short, **if you delay, you pay!**

You must pay your tax bill on time

Payments of tax owed for the April 1996 to April 1997 tax year must be made by **31 January 1998**.

You will be charged interest of 8.5 per cent on late payment of tax or if you pay too little tax. The current rate is 8.5 per cent but this is subject to change. Rates are set to give the Inland Revenue a commercial rate of return – so the rates are not that cheap.

Any tax for the year to April 1997 which is due on 31 January 1998, but is still unpaid as of 28 February 1998 will cost you an extra 5 per cent of the outstanding amount. So you will be surcharged for being as little as one month late. If you still have not paid by 31 July 1998 there is a 10 per cent surcharge.

If you or your accountant is calculating your tax bill, you will know how much to pay. If the Inland Revenue is calculating your tax bill you will be sent a tax demand in November or December – before the 31 January 1998 deadline.

Remember, payments must be received by the Inland Revenue by the deadline. This means you will have to pay your tax bill at least three days earlier to make sure it arrives on time. You can do this by paying your bill by Bank Giro at any branch of your bank. If you have been sent a tax assessment, a payment *payslip* will be attached to the bottom of the form. Allow three working days for your cheque to clear. When you pay your tax bill, your bank will stamp the top part of the form (which you keep) to show how much you paid and when you paid it.

If you are paying by post, allow three to four days for the cheque to reach the Inland Revenue. Payments should be made to the Accounts Office, not your Tax Office. Even if you are calculating your own tax bill, the Inland Revenue will send you a reminder towards the end of the year and a *payslip*. This will tell you where to send your cheque. For security reasons make your cheque payable to 'INLAND REVENUE ONLY' and after this write your tax reference number. Make sure your cheque is cross 'A/C PAYEE'. However, if you send in your cheque by post you will not be given a receipt.

You can also pay your tax bill at post offices, in which case the cheque should be made payable to Post Office Counters Ltd.

PREPARING TO FILL IN YOUR TAX RETURN

If you are sent a Tax Return you **must** fill it in and return it on time. The Tax Return is used to assess the amount of Income Tax and Capital Gains Tax you owe as well as National Insurance if you are self-employed or in partnership.

HOW EASY WILL IT BE TO FILL IN MY TAX RETURN?

Half of the work involved is in the preparation. If you have the right paperwork – such as tax forms given to you by your employer – filling in your Tax Return should be fairly straightforward. You simply have to copy information from documents you should already have into the boxes on your Tax Return.

More than eight in ten people will get the same length Tax Return or a shorter version than they received last year. So for most people there will be very little extra paperwork. Some half a million taxpayers will no longer get a Tax Return. These are taxpayers who only need to change their tax allowances or reclaim tax deducted from savings interest. They will be able to do this without filling in a Tax Return.

Most taxpayers may only have to fill in around 40 boxes on their Tax Return although the self-employed may have to fill in at least double that number. How much work you have to do will depend on how many pages of forms there are in your indivdual Tax Return. In addition to the main eight pages there are a further 22 pages covering different types of income from rents to share schemes. It is unlikely that you will need all of these.

A lot of the work involved in filling in your Tax Return will still have to be done even if you employ an accountant. You will have to collect all the relevant paperwork, keep records and know what information to give your accountant. If you do not, your accountant may not be able to fill in your Tax Return correctly or on time. Employing an accountant is highly advisable if you have complicated tax affairs. But you cannot tax deduct the costs unless you are self-employed and use an accountant to prepare your accounts.

WARNING: Anyone can set up in business as a tax adviser. Always check the qualifications of anyone you employ to help you fill in your Tax Return. Remember, you are liable if there are any errors.

HOW DO I KNOW IF I HAVE THE RIGHT FORMS?

Included at the end of your main eight-page Tax Return will be any extra pages that you need for your different types of income and profits. **You must check that you have the right pages.** You will be able to do this when you fill in the questionnaire on page 2 of your Tax Return. In trials of the new Self Assessment system, the Inland Revenue found that over half of the Tax Returns that were incomplete were wrong because taxpayers were missing the correct pages.

You will also have Inland Revenue Guidance Notes on how to fill in your Tax Return and you can ask for extra Help Sheets if you need more information or advice. A list of Help Sheets is on the front of each set of Guidance Notes. If you are missing any extra pages or want Help Sheets sent to you, ring the Orderline on 0645 000 404.

WHAT IF I HAVE NOT GOT ALL THE FIGURES I NEED?

If for some reason the information you require is not available or you cannot get an accurate figure, you can enter your best estimate. You must clearly mark it as an estimate and once you have obtained the accurate figure you must tell the Inland Revenue.

WHAT IF I MAKE A MISTAKE ON MY TAX RETURN?

When you send back your Tax Return the Inland Revenue will check it for obvious mistakes, for instance, you forgot to sign it or did not include the correct paperwork. The Self Assessment rules allow for human error. *You can amend your Tax Return and tax assessment provided you do this within 12 months of the date you sent it back.* In most cases you will not be charged a penalty. However, you may be charged interest on tax you should have paid earlier.

HOW WILL THE INLAND REVENUE CHECK THAT I AM PAYING THE RIGHT AMOUNT OF TAX?

The Inland Revenue will be doing spot checks on Tax Returns to make sure that taxpayers are not abusing Self Assessment in order to pay less tax. Some 100,000 of the 4.5 million self-employed will face random audits and 1–2 per cent of all taxpayers will have their tax affairs investigated.

Every Tax Return will be input into a computer and the calculations checked. So, even if you have calculated your own tax bill, the tax office will double-check the figures. While the Tax Returns are being input into the computer tax inspectors will use what is called their 'nose' – their instinct for spotting errors and those trying to evade tax.

If you have calculated the tax you owe under the new Self Assessment guidelines yourself and you have made a mistake, the Inland Revenue will send you an amended calculation and a tax demand if necessary. If you disagree with any correction made, you can and should challenge it.

If the Inland Revenue decides it wants to investigate your tax affairs it will do so within 12 months of the date you sent in your Tax Return. That is why it is essential to keep records. An enquiry can range from a straightforward question about how you have added up your figures to a full investigation. If you are selected for an enquiry you will be sent information telling you what to expect.

The Inland Revenue will also double check your figures against other information from your employer, bank or building society and other income sources. All savings interest over £250 a year is reported to the Inland Revenue, so you cannot escape paying higher rate tax on this.

If the Inland Revenue has demanded too much tax it will give you a rebate and pay you 4 per cent interest (although this rate can change in line with interest rates). If the Inland Revenue demands too much tax 'on account' you can challenge this by filling in form SA303.

HOW TO GET THE INLAND REVENUE TO HELP YOU

If you want help, advice or an information leaflet, ring the Inland Revenue – the telephone number of your tax office is printed on the top of your Tax Return. Or you can telephone your local Tax Enquiry Centre – the number is in the phone book. The switchboard will be open to the public from 9am to 4.30pm and most offices are open for you to visit for at least eight hours a day. A Helpline is also open until 10pm on weekdays and from 8am to 10pm at weekends. The telephone number is 0645 000 444.

The Inland Revenue has several leaflets to help you. You can get copies by ringing the Orderline on 0645 000 404. It is open between 8am and 10pm every day including weekends (but not Christmas Day). Remember, Inland Revenue leaflets and advice are **free**.

❑ If you write to the Inland Revenue quote your tax reference number – it is printed on your notice of income tax code, statement of account and Tax Return.

CAN I USE A COMPUTER TO HELP ME FILL IN MY TAX RETURN?

You may have seen computer packages advertised. These may help you to work out your tax bill. However, if there is an error on your Tax Return you cannot use your computer as an excuse.

The Inland Revenue has its own computer package, but it will only cover the basic eight-page Tax Return and the extra pages covering employment.

A BEGINNER'S GUIDE TO INCOME TAX

This section will help you to understand:

❏ why you are filling in certain boxes on your Tax Return;
❏ how the figures are worked out;
❏ which items and figures you do not have to include on your Tax Return.

The following chapters look at Income Tax because this is the main tax covered by your Tax Return. **Capital Gains Tax**, the tax on profits from the sale of shares, investments, second homes and other assets is covered in Chapter 9 of Section 4. The other 'tax' assessed using the Tax Return is **National Insurance, if you are self-employed**. Details of the rates for the self-employed are included in Chapter 4 of Section 4 on self-employment.

This book looks at the rates in the tax year 6 April 1996 to 5 April 1997 – the year covered by the Tax Return sent out in April 1997.

WHAT INCOME DO I HAVE TO INCLUDE ON MY TAX RETURN?

Income tax is only payable on taxable income and you do not have to pay tax on all of your income – some types of income are tax free. **You do not have to include the following on your Tax Return.**

Tax-free income:

❑ Income from National Savings Certificates.
❑ The first £70 of interest from National Savings Bank Ordinary Accounts.
❑ Premium bond prizes.
❑ Proceeds from most life insurance policies.
❑ Save-As-You-Earn interest.
❑ Profit-related pay up to a maximum of £4000 or 20% of your pay if this is lower.
❑ Income from Personal Equity Plans (PEPs).
❑ Redundancy pay (up to £30,000) and certain other payments when you lose a job.
❑ Shares allocated to you by your employer under an approved share incentive scheme.
❑ Local authority home improvement grants.
❑ Most educational grants and scholarships.
❑ Maintenance payments paid by your former spouse or the father of your children are tax free up to certain limits.
❑ Some employee benefits such as a subsidised canteen (see Chapter 2 on employment in Section 4 for more details).
❑ Some social security benefits including:
  - child benefit and child care allowances;
  - housing benefits;
  - maternity allowance but not maternity pay;
  - sickness benefit;
  - family credit;
  - income support (in most cases);
  - invalidity pensions;
  - war widows pension;
  - disability living allowance;
  - widow's payment;
  - job release allowance to men aged 64 and over or women aged 59 and over;
  - attendance allowance;
  - severe disablement allowance;
  - Christmas bonus for pensioners;
  - industrial injury benefits.

And the following do not count as income and so are not taxed:

❏ Prizes and betting winnings including from the National Lottery, competitions and gambling.

❏ Gifts and presents (but not if they are for work done).

NB: If you sell something the proceeds do not count as income but may be liable for Capital Gains Tax – the tax you pay on the profit you make when you sell an asset like shares, investments, second homes and businesses (but not personal possessions).

If you inherit money or assets these do not count as income and as such are not taxed. However, if interest was earned on the estate (the amount of wealth and assets left by someone when they die) while that estate was being administered, you may have to pay tax on that income.

INCOME TAX RATES AND TAX BANDS

Income Tax is charged at three different *tax rates* on income that falls into different *tax bands*. You only pay each rate of income tax on income that falls within a particular tax band. This means that you can pay tax at the lower rate, basic rate and higher rate if you have income in each of these tax bands.

The amount of tax charged on each tax band has been calculated for you. *These income bands are in addition to your tax allowance – so you only pay tax on income above your allowance. The income covered by your allowance is tax free regardless of your rate of tax.*

Table 3.1 *Income Tax: the different tax rates and tax bands*

Tax rate	%	Income Tax band Tax year 6 April 1996 to 5 April 1997	Tax you will have to pay
Lower	20%	The first **£3900** of taxable income in excess of your allowances	(20% of £3900) **£780**
Basic	24%	The next **£3901** to **£25,500** of taxable income (£21,599 of income)	(24% of £21,599) **£5183.76**
Higher	40%	Taxable income in excess of **£25,500**	40% on income above this limit

TAX ALLOWANCES

You do not have to pay tax on all of your income, profits or wealth. You are entitled to what is called a *tax allowance* – the amount you can earn **before** you have to pay tax. The allowances you will receive automatically or can claim are:

❑ **Personal allowance:** Everyone has a personal allowance – but you are only allowed one. If you have more than one job or are an employee and self-employed, you can only set the personal allowance against one source of income – usually the main source of income.

❑ **Married couple's allowance:** To qualify for the married couple's allowance you must be married and living with your spouse. You can still be regarded as living with your spouse even if you are not living under the same roof as long as you are still married and neither of you intends to make the separation permanent. **The married couple's allowance is in addition to your personal allowance.** If you marry after 5 April 1996 you will be entitled to one-twelfth of the married couple's allowance for each month of your marriage for the April 1996 to April 1997 tax year. It is given to the husband. The wife can claim half without her husband's consent and all of it with his agreement.

❑ **Age allowance:** The personal allowance rises with age. To qualify for an age allowance you must have reached either 65 or 75 by the end of the tax year, 5 April 1997. The married couple's age allowance is also increased if either one of the couple is aged 65 or over at the end of the tax year.

❑ **Widow's bereavement allowance:** A widow is entitled to this in the year of her husband's death and in the following tax year.

❑ **Single parent allowance:** This is officially called the 'additional personal allowance'. It is given to those who are single, separated, divorced or widowed and who have a child living with them; or to those living with a wife who is unable to look after herself throughout the tax year because of disability or illness.

❑ **Blind person's allowance:** This is given to those who are registered blind.

How allowances reduce your tax bill

Your tax allowance is how much you can earn **before** paying tax, **not** the amount of tax you save. How much tax you save depends on your top rate of tax.

The personal tax allowance means that you do not have to pay tax on £3765 of taxable income in the April 1996 to April 1997 tax year. So you save the tax you would have had to pay on that proportion of your income.

If you would normally pay 24 per cent tax on that £3765 of income, you save:

$$24\% \text{ of } £3,765 = £903.60$$

However, if you are a higher rate taxpayer and pay 40 per cent tax on your highest earnings, your savings will be as follows:

$$40\% \text{ of } £3765 = \textbf{£1506}$$

But you can only save 40 per cent tax on income taxed at 40 per cent. So, if you only have £2000 of earnings taxed in the higher rate tax bracket, you will save 40 per cent on that £2000 only. Your savings on the remaining allowance of £1765 will be at the basic tax rate of 24 per cent.

Some allowances have *relief restrictions*, which means that the rate of tax relief is restricted to a certain rate of tax as in the case of the *married couple's allowance*. This means that instead of saving up to 40 per cent of the allowance you can only save 15 per cent.

SPECIAL RULES FOR PENSIONERS

The age allowance given to those aged 65 and over has an *earnings restriction*. This means that if you had a **total** gross income (before tax is deducted) of more than £15,200 in the April 1996 to April 1997 tax year your allowances would be reduced by £1 for every £2 you earned over this limit. The allowance only stops being reduced when it falls below the basic personal allowance of £3750. So the more you earn the less tax savings you make. Exclude tax free income from your total income. This works as follows:

Pensioner A is 67 and has a total income from pensions and investments in the April 1996 to April 1997 tax year of **£18,000.** (Add tax deducted from income to that income to give the gross figure.)

His age increased personal allowance (because he is over 65) is **£4910.**

But he can only earn **£15,200** before this allowance is reduced by £1 for every £2 he earns above this limit. So his allowance will be reduced as follows:

£18,000 (his income) − **£15,200** (the restriction) = **£2800.**
So he earns £2800 more than the restriction.
The allowance is reduced by £1 for every £2 of earnings over the restriction.
So £2800 ÷ 2 = **£1400.**

So his allowance will be reduced by £1400.
£4910 (his age allowance) − **£1400** (the reduction as a result of the earnings restriction) = **£3510.**

However, this reduced allowance of £3510 is below the basic personal allowance of £3765.

So his basic personal allowance will be £3765.

So instead of reducing his allowance by **£1400** he has only reduced it by **£1145.**
So he still has not used up £1400 − £1145 = **£255** of the reduction.

If you are married and do not use up the earnings reduction on your personal age allowance, the extra reduction is taken away from your married couple's allowance. If you are not married, no further reduction is made. However, in Pensioner A's case his married couple's allowance will be reduced by £255.

For a full listing of tax allowances and resultant tax savings, see Table 3.2.

TAX CODES

Tax Codes are given to those who receive income under PAYE (Pay-As-You-Earn) which is the system for collecting taxes from wages and salaries and company pensions. The code adjusts your *tax allowances* so a greater or lesser amount of tax can be deducted from your salary or company pension before it is paid to you. This enables the Inland Revenue to collect any extra tax. **Your tax code is your responsibility and it is up to you to check that your code is correct.**

Table 3.2 *Tax allowances for the tax year April 1996 – April 1997 (including tax savings as a result of allowances) and April 1997–April 1998 allowances*

Type of allowance	1996/97 allowance	Amount of tax saving for basic rate taxpayer and rate at which tax savings are made	Amount of tax saving for higher rate taxpayer and rate at which tax savings are made	1997/98 allowance
Standard personal allowance	£3765	£903.60 (at 24%)	£1506.00 (at 40%)	£4045
Standard married couple's allowance*	£1790	£268.50 (at 15%)	£268.50 (at 15%)	£1830
Aged 65 to 74: personal allowance	£4910	£1178.40 (at 24%)	£1964.00 (at 40%)	£5220
Aged 65 to 74: married couple's allowance*	£3115	£467.25 (at 15%)	£467.25 (at 15%)	£3185
Aged 75 and over: personal allowance	£5090	£1221.60 (at 24%)	£2036.00 (at 40%)	£5400
Aged 75 and over: married couple's allowance*	£3155	£437.25 (at 15%)	£473.25 (at 15%)	£3225
Additional relief for single parents*	£1790	£268.50 (at 15%)	£268.50 (at 15%)	£1830
Widow's bereavement allowance*	£1790	£268.50 (at 15%)	£268.50 (at 15%)	£1830
Blind person's allowance	£1250	£300.00 (at 24%)	£500.00 (at 40%)	£1280
Income limit for age-related allowances **	£15,200			£15,600

Notes

* Relief restricted to 15 per cent – this means that regardless of the tax rate you pay you can only get a tax saving at 15 per cent. This is to restrict the tax advantage and to make it the same for all taxpayers.

** Age allowances reduced by £1 for every £2 income in excess of the limit until the standard allowance is reached. So if you earn £1000 over the limit your age allowance will be reduced by £500.

You may be sent a PAYE Coding Notice by the Inland Revenue every year or when your circumstances change. This will tell you what the Code is. You may also be able to find your tax code on your wage slip or your P45 (if you have lost your job or are moving jobs).

The code is made up of numbers (usually three) and a letter, for example:

312H, K311

The figures in your Code show the amount you can earn in the tax year before paying tax.

When working out your Tax Code the last number is deleted. So if you can earn £3765 before paying tax your code will have the number 376 (one-tenth of your net allowances rounded down). The letter next to these numbers tells your employer what type of taxpayer you are.

The numbers

The Inland Revenue adds up your allowances including the personal allowance and married couple's allowance as well as any tax relief you are due for personal pension plan contributions.

Then it adds up any deductions. You pay tax on your employee perks and benefits (such as your company car) by an adjustment in your Tax Code. You are taxed on the value of these perks. Untaxed interest (interest received gross), tax on part-time earnings and property income can also be collected through your tax code, as can any outstanding tax from previous years.

The Inland Revenue subtracts the amount of *deductions* from the amount of *allowances* to work out a final figure. It may also deduct an allowance restriction which enables it to restrict the married couple's allowance to 15%. The last number is then knocked off. This is the number in your tax code.

The letters

These tell your employer how to treat your allowances and the type of taxpayer you are. This is what the most commonly used letters mean:

L   You get the basic personal allowance – normally a single person with no employee benefits.

H   You get the personal allowance and the married couple's allowance – normally given to those with no employee benefits.

P   You get the higher age-related personal allowance for those aged between 65 and 74.

V   You get the higher age-related married couple's allowance and higher personal allowance for those aged between 65 and 74.

T   If you have a T code your tax will not be adjusted by your employer but by the Tax Office. You get a T code if: your age-related allowance is reduced because your income is more than the £15,200 limit; you are 75 and over during the tax year and get the higher age allowance and higher married couple's allowance; you do not want your employer to know your age or marital status; you have benefits in kind which are altered each year.

K   You get the K code if the value of any perks of your job and other deductions are greater than your personal allowances. The extra tax will be collected each month through PAYE, so you do not have to pay a big bill at the end of the tax year. See 'The K code' below.

The K code

This means that you have a negative allowance, ie your deductions are greater than your allowances. It not only means that *all* your income is taxed (you have no tax free allowance) but also that you have to pay an extra amount of tax from your salary. For example:

Mr R has total allowances of	**£1880**
His total deductions are	**£5000**
So he has a **negative** amount of allowance for the tax year of	**–£3120**

He is paid monthly so the £3120 is divided by 12 = **£260**

Every month he will pay tax on **all** his salary plus a further £260 of tax will be deducted from his pay.

A booklet 'Understanding Your Tax Code' which comes with your Coding Notice will explain how your tax code is worked out. If you still need further information telephone the number on the top of your Coding Notice.

If you receive State benefits or a State pension

If you are taxed under PAYE and also receive taxable State benefits tax due on these may be collected through PAYE. So if you receive an employer's pension you may also have to pay taxes on your State pension and other benefits through your tax code.

TAX RELIEF

Tax relief reduces your tax bill by refunding tax you have already paid or by cost of items which qualify for tax relief. Sometimes tax relief is given automatically so you do not notice that you are getting a rebate. In other cases you have to claim the tax relief on your Tax Return.

For example, if you are a higher rate taxpayer you will get tax relief of 40p for every £1 you put in your pension. But you can only get tax relief at 40 per cent if you pay tax at 40 per cent. So, if you want to claim tax relief at 40 per cent on £1000 invested in your pension but you only have £600 of earnings taxed at 40 per cent the Inland Revenue will only give you top rate tax relief on the £600. You will get basic rate tax relief of 24 per cent on the remaining £400 you invest.

You can get *full tax relief* which means you get tax back at your highest rate of tax on all of the outgoings. Or you can get *restricted tax relief* where the tax reduction is only allowed on a proportion of the outgoings. There is also *reduced rate tax relief* which restricts the rate of tax relief – so if you pay tax at 40 per cent you may only be able to claim the tax relief at 15 per cent.

You do not always have to claim tax relief. Sometimes you get *tax relief at source*. This happens with your home loan on your only or main property. Most mortgages come under MIRAS (*mortgage interest tax relief at source*). Your mortgage lender will automatically give you *tax relief* on your mortgage payments up to the *tax relief limit* of £30,000 and will give you this tax relief at the correctly *reduced* rate of 15 per cent. This tax relief means your mortgage payments are automatically reduced. If your mortgage is not covered by MIRAS you will have to claim the tax relief on your Tax Return.

FILLING IN YOUR
TAX RETURN

THE MAIN TAX RETURN
PAGES 1 AND 2

Read the cover of your Tax Return to make sure you fully understand what is required. *Everyone has to fill in page 2* to make sure they have the right supplementary pages.

Q1: EMPLOYMENT

Tick the *yes* box if you were employed at any time during the tax year 6 April 1996 to 5 April 1997. You may be classed as an employee even if you only do casual work.

⇒ If you are unsure about whether or not you were an employee check to see if you have a P60 – the form given out by employers by 31 May each year detailing your income and tax. If you have one, you were an employee.

⇒ If you did have a job, but are now unemployed or self-employed, did that job end after 6 April 1996? If it did, tick the *yes* box. You should have a P45.

⇒ The term office holder means that you held an office, for example company secretary.

⇒ Agency workers, those who worked on a casual or contract basis with that work arranged by an agency and with tax deducted from their pay, are also classed as employees.

⇒ If you worked on a casual basis – even though you are normally self-employed – and worked in a company's office and were paid to work, not for work done, you will *also* be classed as an employee.

Q2: SHARE OPTIONS

Before you tick either the *yes* or *no* box you must first find out if your income from share options or share schemes is *taxable*. Share option schemes are set up by your employer to enable you to buy shares in the company. Most share option schemes are **not** taxable. Read the following notes for guidance.

⇒ If you have share options granted under an approved savings-related share option scheme and your money is invested in a Save-As-You-Earn (SAYE) account to buy the shares at the end of five years, you do **not** have any taxable income. Tick the *no* box.

⇒ However, if you invested in a SAYE scheme and exercised the option (bought shares) within three years and you did so because the company you work for was sold or taken over, you **do** have to complete the share scheme pages. Tick the *yes* box.

⇒ Approved profit-sharing scheme shares held by trustees for three years do **not** have to be included.

⇒ If your share options were not in an approved Inland Revenue share option scheme you should tick the *yes* box. Check on the scheme documents for the word 'approved'.

⇒ Approved executive share options granted to you before 17 July 1995 do **not** have to be included either, provided that the option is exercised (ie you get the shares) between three and ten years after the option was granted, and provided you do not take shares within three years of exercising (buying) other share options. If this is the case tick the *no* box.

⇒ You **do** have to include approved executive share options if the options were granted after 17 July 1995 and the total value of all shares you have subject to option was more than £30,000 at the time these new options were granted.

⇒ You should also tick the *yes* box if you received payment for giving up, or for not exercising, a share option.

⇒ Although you may not have to declare any of these share schemes as income, you may have to declare them as a capital gain (see Q 9 in this section on capital gains).

⇒ Do **not** tick the *yes* box if you only received dividends from shares bought through a company share scheme. These go on page 3 of your main Tax Return.

Q3: SELF-EMPLOYMENT

You may have received earnings from self-employment even though you do not think of yourself as being self-employed. Read the following notes.

⇒ You were self-employed if you worked for yourself – carried on a trade, profession or vocation – arranging your own work, deciding when you work, providing your own tools and equipment and invoicing someone else or another business for the work you did.

⇒ You may also have income from self-employment if you received payments from a company without tax being deducted from this income first. For instance, you may have been given commission for introducing business to a company or worked on a freelance basis.

⇒ You can be self-employed and an employee.

⇒ If you make money out of your hobby – for instance, you buy antiques, repair and renovate them and sell them on for a profit – you may also be classed as self-employed as you are carrying out a trade.

⇒ You must tick the *yes* box if you were self-employed at any time during the tax year from 6 April 1996 to 5 April 1997.

⇒ If you ran your own business but are a director of it then you will be classed as an employee, not as self-employed.

Q4: PARTNERSHIPS

If you are or were a partner of a business at any time during the tax year from 6 April 1996 to 5 April 1997, you may have drawn up or signed a partnership agreement. If not, and you were in business with one or more others to share the profits and the risks of that business, you will be classed as being in partnership.

Q5: LAND AND PROPERTY

Some income from land and property does **not** have to be included in this section.

⇒ If you run a bed and breakfast business or rent out rooms and provide extra services such as meals in your only or main home, your activities will amount to a trade and as such you should tick the *no* box. These come under self-employment.

⇒ Even if you are making the most of the Rent a Room relief – which allows you to rent a room in your home for up to £3250 a year and get that income tax free – you should tick the *yes* box.

⇒ If you receive rent from letting out your overseas holiday home this is covered in the foreign income section (this section only covers UK land and property).

Q6: FOREIGN

This includes any overseas pensions or benefits, income from foreign companies or savings institutions, offshore funds or overseas trusts, rents from land and property, foreign life insurance policies and annuities.

⇒ If you invest in a UK unit trust or investment trust that in turn invests in overseas companies, this is **not** classed as foreign earnings.

⇒ Tick the *yes* box if you want to claim relief for foreign tax that has been deducted on any income or gains – this includes overseas earnings if you are *self-employed.*

⇒ *Even if you did not receive income from overseas in 1996–1997, but you did in 1995–1996, you may still have to fill in these forms.* If you acquired the investment, property or savings before 6 April 1994 and still owned them last year, you should tick the *yes* box and see the notes that come with your Foreign pages.

⇒ Tick the *yes* box if you received income from renting out your overseas home.

Q7: TRUSTS

The *yes* box must be ticked if you were a beneficiary or received money from a trust fund. If you created (were the settlor) of a trust you must also tick *yes*. But if you received a legacy in trust (from the estate of a deceased person), tick the *no* box.

⇒ If you receive income from a 'nominee' account or a bare trust do not include this here. For tax purposes the income and profits belong to you and not to the trust. Include this income on the relevant pages of your main Tax Return – so shares in a 'nominee' account should be included in the shares and dividends section.

⇒ If you receive money as a legacy and it is held in trust, include the income in the relevant section – rents from property in land & property and interest from building societies in the savings section.

Q8: CAPITAL GAINS

Before you can tick the *yes* or *no* boxes you have to know what capital gains are. This is a tax on profits when you sell assets, investments, businesses or land. Instead of being taxed on the income you are taxed on the profits (Capital Gains) when you sell an asset for more than you bought it for.

Did you sell your home?

Exempt means it was your only or main home and you have not used it for business. As such, profits made when you sell your home are exempt from tax. If you sold your home during the tax year tick the *yes* box. But this does **not** mean that you have to pay Capital Gains Tax or that you have to fill in the Capital Gains form. You may only have to do this if you sold some land, earned money from your home by renting it out, or used your home for running a business.

Did you dispose of other chargeable assets worth more than £12,600 in total?

You will only know the answer to this once you know what *chargeable assets* are. The following guidelines should help.

⇒ Stocks and shares, land, second homes, antiques and works of art. Most assets that are an investment are included.

⇒ You do *not* have to declare: personal possessions or chattels (which are each worth £6000 or less when you 'dispose' of them), profits from selling your car (unless you sell cars for a business), Personal Equity Plans (PEPs), bonuses from TESSA accounts, Gilts (UK Government stocks), foreign currency for personal use, betting and lottery winnings, most life insurance policies and some National Savings Investments. And if you are running a business, trading stock that you sell is also exempt.

⇒ The £12,600 applies to the total value of these items sold or disposed of during the tax year, not to each individual item.

⇒ The Inland Revenue uses the word 'dispose' rather than sold, because you must also declare assets given as gifts or exchanged.

⇒ If you sold a business or business asset or made a capital gain within a partnership and made an individual profit of more than £12,600 in total, tick the *yes* box.

⇒ You do not have to pay Capital Gains Tax on money you receive as a gift (as opposed to assets you give) or on money (or an asset) which is subject to Income Tax. So there is no capital gains tax on share dividends but there may be when you sell the shares for a profit.

Were your gains/profits more than £6300?

This means that you sold your assets or investments at a profit – and that the profit from all the items you sold is more than £6300.

⇒ To work out the 'gain' or profit write down the price you sold it for and then deduct the price you paid for it (or its market value when you received it) – the remainder is the profit. You can then deduct the costs of buying and selling the asset, costs in enhancing its value (such as restoration costs) and a set allowance for inflation. If you are still in doubt as to whether or not you made gains over £6300 see Chapter 9 in this section on Capital Gains.

⇒ Remember the £6300 limit is for your total gains, not each individual gain, during the tax year.

⇒ If you made a loss you should also fill in the Capital Gains Tax section so that you can offset these losses against any profits in the current tax year or in future tax years. This will reduce the amount of tax you have to pay.

Q9: NON-RESIDENCE

This will apply to you if you live abroad full-time or for most of the year. If you have not lived or worked overseas tick the *no* box.

⇒ If you spend less than 183 days in the UK in any tax year and, over four years an average of less than 91 days, or you have spent the entire year overseas then you are generally classed as a non-resident.

⇒ Ordinary residence applies to those who intend to make – or have made – their home abroad on a more permanent basis.

⇒ Domicile is more permanent still – you have to show that you have no intention of returning to the UK.

⇒ If you live and work in more than one country in a tax year you tick the *yes* box and fill in the questionnaire that comes with the non-residence pages. You should also fill in the Foreign pages to make sure you are not taxed in more than one country.

⇒ If you are living in the UK but come from or usually live overseas, tick the *yes* box.

STEP 2: FILL IN THE SUPPLEMENTARY PAGES

Only fill in those pages that you have said you need to by ticking 'yes' in boxes Q1 to Q9. If you ticked a box – for example, self-employment – but do not have the right supplementary pages then ring the Orderline on 0645 000 404 and ask for any missing forms.

As you only have to fill in those forms that relate to your individual circumstances and these will vary from reader to reader, you do not have to read the Chapters between 2 and 10 that do not relate to you. Once you have read the relevant chapters go straight to Chapter 11, which tells you how to fill in the remaining pages, 3–8, of your main Tax Return.

You need to fill in the supplementary pages **before** filling in the rest of your Tax Return. If you do not you may not be able to fill in the remaining pages correctly.

Remember also that you must fill in the Tax Return in blue or black ink. However, do not forget that if you are worried about making a mistake, you can use pencil. Then, when you are happy with the figures, you can write over them in ink.

The Tax Return states 'ignore pence'. This simply means that you can round all income figures down. For instance instead of writing £109.78 you simply write £109. Do not round up to £110 unless it works to your advantage – so round up your outgoings.

EMPLOYMENT

These two pages of the Tax Return should be filled in by those who were in PAYE employment during the tax year from 6 April 1996 to 5 April 1997. **A different form has to be filled in for each period of employment.** So if you have had three different jobs during the year, you will need to fill in three different forms.

📄 PAPERWORK REQUIRED

You will need the following:

- ❑ Your P60 Certificate of Pay. This shows how much Income Tax and National Insurance contributions you have paid. Your employer should give this to you by 31 May 1997. If you had more than one job, your pay from that previous job will be included on your P60.
- ❑ If you left a job during the tax year, your P45 (Part 1A).
- ❑ Also, your P11D, P9D or other information from your employer about benefits and expenses (such as company cars). This should be given to you by your employer by 6 July 1997.
- ❑ Your notice of tax coding if you have been sent one by the Inland Revenue. This will tell you the employee benefits on which you are paying tax.
- ❑ Details of any business expenses.
- ❑ Your pay slips if you are missing any of the above forms.

Most figures have only to be copied from the documents listed above. If you have more than one figure to fit into each box, you will have to add up the figures. So have a calculator to hand.

Tax dates: Last year you had to send your tax back by 31 October 1996 and pay tax by then or by 1 December 1996.. This year you must send your tax return back and pay tax by 31 January 1998.

DETAILS OF EMPLOYER: BOXES 1.1 TO 1.7

1.1 and 1.2: Employer's PAYE reference and name

Copy the name and reference number on your P60 or Part 1A of your P45.

1.3: Date employment started

Only fill this in if you started a new job in the tax year between 6 April 1996 and 5 April 1997. If not, leave it blank.

1.4: Date finished

Only fill this in if you stopped working during the tax year. Copy the date listed on Part 1A of your P45.

1.5: Employer's address

Again, copy the one listed on your P60.

1.6: Company directors

Tick this if you were employed as a director of a company during the tax year.

1.7: Directors of a close company

You should know if your company is a close (or closed) company but if you do not, this generally means a company that is under the control of its directors (where the directors are also shareholders) or companies with five or fewer shareholders. If you are still in doubt ask your tax office for guidance.

INCOME FROM EMPLOYMENT: BOXES 1.8 TO 1.11

> **M**oney: Remember, only include pay received in the 6 April 1996 to 5 April 1997 tax year.

1.8: Payments

This is listed as total pay on your P60 (or P45). If there is more than one figure, the one you need is 'net pay after superannuation' (you do not pay tax on earnings invested in your company pension scheme) or 'total pay this employment'. Make sure charitable payroll giving is also excluded. If you had more than one job or were unemployed there may be figures in the 'previous employment' box. These should not be included on this form – remember you need to have a separate form for each type of employment.

> **W**arning: Take care if you were unemployed during the year. Unemployment benefit, income support or jobseeker's allowance may be included in the 'pay from previous employment' box on your P60. Do not include these as part of your salary. Any unemployment or other benefit should be deducted from your 'previous pay' figure and put in box **11.5** on your Tax Return.

Your payments figure in box **1.8** should include wages, statutory sick pay and maternity pay (if paid by your employer), commissions, overtime, fees and bonuses.

Special notes for employees
You must include all the income received in the tax year as an employee even if you earned it in an earlier tax year or you have been paid in advance for work not yet done. You should also include pay that you were entitled to receive but have not yet been paid.

Special notes for directors
All income received in the tax year must be included even if you

earned the money in an earlier tax year or have been paid for work not yet done. You should also include sums that were due to you but which you arranged to receive in some other way. Payment is treated as being received on the earliest of the following: the date you were paid or payment on account was made; the date you became entitled to be paid or paid on account even if you were paid later; the date money was credited to you in the company's accounts or records even if you were not able to draw on the money at the time.

1.9 and 1.10: Other payments

These include tips and any other payments not included on the P60 (or P45 Part 1A or your payslips). Do **not** include redundancy or certain other lump-sum payments on termination of employment, expenses, loans or money for petrol. Include all income that is from or related to your work but not included in box **1.8**. In box **1.9** you should include tips and gratuities.

> **Warning:** The Inland Revenue has a good idea of the amount of tips given to each type of worker – waiter, hairdresser, taxi driver etc. So, if you try to cheat, this may easily be spotted.

The following *do not have to be included* and should not be included in the figure on your P60:

❑ Profit-related pay – this is tax free up to 20 per cent of your salary or £4000 a year, whichever is the lower.
❑ Contributions to the company pension scheme.
❑ Payroll giving (money taken from your pay and given to charity).
❑ Gifts that are genuinely presents (not instead of pay for work). They must cost your employer £100 or less.
❑ Gifts to mark a personal event such as marriage.

1.11: Tax deducted

Write in the amount of tax deducted from your payments in boxes **1.8** to **1.10**. You should find this figure on your P60 (or P45). If you had tax refunded put the amount in brackets.

EMPLOYEE BENEFITS AND EXPENSES: BOXES 1.12 TO 1.23

Benefits (also known as benefits-in-kind) generally mean the perks that go with your job, such as a company car, free private health insurance or a subsidised mortgage. To fill in these boxes, you will need form P11D which will be given to you by your employer by 6 July 1997.

> **W**arning: You must check your P11D carefully as you are responsible for what you enter on your Tax Return and these forms can be incorrect..

Some items may have been left off your P11D – this may be because they are **exempt** from tax (see list on page 41).

Expenses dispensations: what every employee should know

In some cases expenses will *not* be listed on your P11D because your employer has agreed a special *dispensation* with the Inland Revenue. The dispensation covers expenses that you can claim back, because they are incurred doing your job. As there is no benefit to you (you do not gain because all your expenses are legitimately incurred in your job) this is not classed as a benefit for tax purposes. **The dispensation means that you do not have to include these expenses on your Tax Return**. The only figures for expenses you will see are the ones on which you must pay tax. If no expenses are included on your P11D do not fill in the expenses boxes.

If your employer does not have a dispensation you must add up all the expenses you receive and write the figure in the expenses box **1.23**. So that you are not taxed on these expenses as though they were a perk of your job, you then have to add up all the expenses that were 'wholly, exclusively and necessarily' incurred on business and claim them as deductions in boxes **1.32** to **1.35**. In many cases the two figures will be the same and will cancel each other out.

In some cases the Inland Revenue agrees with your employer that minor benefits and expenses can be settled through PAYE.

How benefits are taxed

To help you fill in the boxes below here is a quick guide to the taxation of employee perks – known as *benefits in kind*. Generally all benefits – any perk you get because of your employment – are taxable unless they are exempt (tax free). Tax is always charged at the *highest rate* of income tax you pay and you pay tax on the value of the perk. So if your perk has a taxable *cash equivalent* (often the cost to the employer) of £1000, as a higher-rate taxpayer you will pay £400 tax.

Special rules apply to *employees earning under £8500* – your earnings figure must **include** the value of benefits and expenses. These rules do **not** apply to company directors. Boxes **1.16** to **1.23** do not have to be filled in if you earn under £8500.

How to calculate if you earn £8500 or more? Take your basic salary, add any bonuses, commissions and other financial payments. Then add the taxable value of any benefits – this is also known as the *cash equivalent*. So if you earn £7000 a year and get a company car with a taxable value of £1400, private medical insurance worth £150 and a mobile phone worth £200, you are treated as though you earn £8750 a year. Therefore the tax concessions given to those earning under £8500 do **not** apply to you even though your basic salary is only £7000 a year.

Which employee benefits are tax free?

❑ **Car parking** spaces at or near your place of work.

- ❑ **Canteens** and tea and coffee and also free or cheap meals, provided these are available to all employees (even if the bosses have their own coffee area or restaurant).
- ❑ **Meal/luncheon vouchers** provided they are not worth more than 15p a day.
- ❑ Childcare in a **workplace nursery** but not nursery place vouchers or free places at subsidised nurseries away from the workplace.
- ❑ **Medical check-ups** provided these are routine or paid for by your employer.
- ❑ **Pension scheme contributions** made by your employer into approved company pension schemes.
- ❑ Any **perks that do not cost your employer** money or do not incur an additional cost. For instance, you work for an airline, theatre, bus or train company and your employer gives you a complimentary or subsidised seat.
- ❑ **Sports facilities** provided they are available to employees generally and not restricted to small groups of staff.
- ❑ **Incidental expenses** while you are working away from home – for things like telephone calls home and laundry. You can receive £5 for every night spent away from home on business in the UK and £10 if you are abroad. However, if you get more than this you cannot claim this amount tax free – the **total** amount then becomes taxable.
- ❑ Directors' and employees' **liability insurance** if it is paid by your employer.
- ❑ **Training expenses** if you need to acquire new skills for your job. The expenses can include books, travel to and from the course and the reasonable cost of meals.
- ❑ **Clothes** specially needed for work (but not everyday work clothes) and the cost of cleaning or repairing protective or functional clothing.
- ❑ **Discounts on goods and services** – say for instance you work for a shop and get cheap goods – provided it does not cost your employer any money.
- ❑ **Employee parties and outings** – normally up to £50 per person per year.
- ❑ Fees and **subscriptions to professional bodies** provided the organisation is Inland Revenue approved and you need to be a member for your job.
- ❑ **Personal gifts** on marriage or retirement (but not money on retirement).

❑ **Relocation expenses** are tax free within limits – generally up to £8000 if you have to move home (if it is no longer within reasonable daily travelling distance from your employment). Costs that can be paid for include: removal, legal, estate agency and even the costs of buying new domestic goods if the old ones are not suitable for your new home.

❑ **Season ticket loans** and other interest free or cheap loans up to a total of £5000.

❑ **Life insurance** provided it is part of your company pension scheme.

❑ Some low-rent or rent-free **job-related living accommodation** – if it is necessary for your job (for instance if you are a caretaker) or it enables you to do your job better (for instance, a publican) or you have to live in it for security reasons.

❑ **Long-service awards** if given for service of 20 years or more with the same employer (no more than £20 per year of service – so that is £400 for the minimum 20 years).

❑ Scholarship and **apprenticeship** schemes provided you are enrolled for at least one academic year and attend full-time for an average of at least 20 weeks a year and the amount of payment (including your lodging, travelling and subsistence but excluding tuition fees) is not above £7000. If you receive more, the full amount is taxable.

❑ **Shares** bought cheaply or given for free in your employer's company through an approved company share scheme – these include profit sharing, share option and SAYE (Save-As-You-Earn) share option schemes.

❑ **Staff suggestion schemes** up to an overall maximum of £5000 for the scheme.

❑ **Late night travel costs** from work provided it is after 9pm and public transport is difficult (but this cannot be paid on a regular basis).

❑ Cost of maintaining and repairing **tools and instruments** including musical instruments needed for work.

❑ **Books** needed for work.

❑ Some of the **heating and lighting costs of your home** and some of the telephone bills and other costs if you **have** to use your home for work. You may also be able to claim some of the rent.

Warning: You can no longer write 'as per employer's return' on your Tax Return and expect the Inland Revenue to track down the figures. You must write in all figures yourself.

How the tax on benefits is calculated

Benefits and perks are taxed on their value or cost to the employer – this is known as the *cash equivalent*. If you pay towards the cost of the benefit, the amount you pay is deducted from the taxable value or cash equivalent. In some cases you are taxed on a fixed amount regardless of how much the perk costs your employer. For instance, the cash equivalent or taxable value of mobile phones is a fixed £200.

Warning: The Inland Revenue may ask you to provide receipts or records (particularly for business mileage) to ensure that you are not cheating on your tax.

BOXES 1.12 TO 1.15

1.12: Assets transferred/payments made for you

The assets referred to are anything your employer gives you that can either be converted into cash or sold. You are taxed on either its second-hand value or the cost of the item to your employer – less any amount you paid for it. Employees earning less than £8500 a year (including benefits and expenses) will only be charged tax on the second-hand value. Payments made by your employer should be included on your P11D.

The type of 'assets' that are covered by this box include:

☐ Television sets.
☐ Furniture.
☐ Clothing.

NB: Cars are dealt with later.

The types of 'payments' include:

☐ Your personal telephone bill paid directly to the telephone company.
☐ Your rent paid to your landlord.
☐ Your personal credit card bill paid directly to the credit card company.

1.13: Vouchers, credit cards and tokens

The value of these will be included in your P11D unless your employer has a dispensation. If you use vouchers or credit cards to meet work expenses, the total value should be written here and you can then claim the amount you spent on company or work expenses in boxes **1.32** to **1.35**.

1.14: Living accommodation

Enter in the value of any accommodation you or your family have because of your job. Again, your employer should give you the figure. (See Tax Free Benefits list on page 41 if you are unsure about whether or not your accommodation is taxable).

1.15: Mileage allowances

If you get paid a mileage allowance for using your own car for business journeys this will be tax free provided it is within certain allowed limits. **You only have to enter a figure in this box if you receive more than is allowed** (see Table 4.1). If you do receive more than is allowed you must **enter only the amount in excess of the tax free allowance**.
    If you are in a *Fixed Profit Car Scheme* you should get details of the profit figures from your employer on form P11D. In this case your employer will automatically only pay you a mileage rate agreed by the Inland Revenue. If this rate is above that allowed (see Table 4.1) the excess is the profit. If your employer gives you a profit figure you must write it in this box. If your employer is not in a Fixed Profit Car Scheme, you can calculate whether or not you have to pay tax by using Table 4.1.

Table 4.1 *Tax free mileage allowances 1996 to 1997 for employees using their own car on business*

	Maximum reimbursement per mile	
Engine size	**First 4000 business miles**	**Excess over 4000 business miles**
Up to 1000cc	27p	16p
1001–1500cc	34p	19p
1501–2000cc	43p	23p
over 2000cc	61p	33p

To calculate if you need to put a profit figure in box **1.5** follow this example:

Mr M drives a 2000cc car. He drives 6000 business miles a year. And his company pays him 40p a mile.

40p per mile × 6000 business miles = total received from his employer **£2400**

Under the *mileage allowance* he is allowed:

4000 business miles × **43p** per mile allowed tax free = **£1720**
The remainder of his business miles (over the 4000 limit) can only be claimed at a lower rate (see Table 4.1).
+ **2000** business miles × **23p** per mile allowed tax free = **£460**
Total allowed = **£2,180**

So he has made a profit of £2400 – £2180 = **£220**
This £220 is the figure he should include in box **1.15**

If the mileage allowance you receive is **less** than the amount you are allowed to receive tax free (see Table 4.1) you can claim the extra in box **1.32**.

This is known as the *quick basis* way of calculating your motoring costs because all you need to record is your business mileage. You can opt to claim motoring costs on a more *exact basis* **instead of** the mileage allowance. In this case you will be able to claim the cost of fuel used on business journeys and some of the running costs including maintenance, insurance and road tax. You should keep detailed records of costs and business and private mileage.

To work out the *business proportion* – the amount you can claim back – total up your mileage for the year. Then calculate the miles on business. So if you clocked up 10,000 miles in a year and 2000 of these were business miles your business proportion will be:

$$^{2000}/_{10000} = {}^1/_5$$

So you can deduct one-fifth of your total costs.

> **T**ax tip: Depending on your circumstances, the *exact basis* of calculating motoring costs – although more time-consuming to work out – may be more tax efficient as it calculates the costs of running your car for business use more accurately. Even if your employer is in a Fixed Profit Car Scheme you can opt to calculate your mileage profit on either an exact or a quick basis.

> **T**ax tip: If you do **not** claim a mileage allowance then there are other tax advantages. You will be able to claim for some of the costs of buying the car in box **1.35.**

BOXES 1.16 TO 1.23

You **do not** have to fill in these boxes if you earn under £8500 (for definition and calculation see page 41) unless you were a company director.

1.16 and 1.17: Car and car fuel benefits

Enter the *cash equivalent* of **cars made available to you for private use**. Private use includes driving to and from work. **Company cars are taxed at 35 per cent of the list price at the time the car was registered** and this value includes accessories. The tax applies to cars provided to you or a member of your family. So if your car has a list price of £10,000 you will be taxed on the taxable value or benefit to you, known as the *cash equivalent*, which will be 35 per cent of £10,000 = £3500.

The maximum price of the car under these rules is £80,000. If you make a contribution towards the cost of buying the car the amount you pay (up to a maximum of £5000) can be deducted from the initial price before calculating the cash equivalent.

If you get free fuel for **private travel** you will also have to include the benefit value of this. If you use your own car for travelling on business (but not to and from work) you can claim this as an expense (see box **1.32**). **Do not include cars that are for business use only – such as pool cars.** If you pay your employer for all the private use of your car you may not have to pay tax.

Your tax is **reduced** if you frequently use your car for business – rather than as a perk. This reduction is based on your *business mileage,* or the number of miles you drive on company business during the tax year from 6 April to 5 April. That is why it is essential that you keep a record of your mileage when you drive your car on company business.

Reducing company car tax
Table 4.2 illustrates the ways in which company car tax can be reduced.

Table 4.2   *How company car tax can be reduced*

Reason for company car tax reduction	Amount of reduction
If you drive between 2500 and 17,900 business miles in the tax year	The taxable value of your car is reduced by one-third
If you drive more than 18,000 business miles in the tax year	The taxable value of your car is reduced by two-thirds (this replaces the one-third figure above)
If your car was over four years old at the end of the tax year (5 April 1997)	The taxable value of your car is reduced by one-third
If you pay your employer for private use of your company car	The taxable value is reduced by the amount you pay your employer
If you have use of the car for only part of the year	The taxable value is reduced by the proportion of the year you had use of the car (so if it was six months it will be reduced by half)

If you are disabled and the car has been modified to meet your special needs	Reduced by costs of installing accessories specifically designed for the disabled

However, if your car is over four years old, giving you a one-third reduction in your company car tax *and* you qualify for a tax reduction because of the business mileage you drive, you must do the following calculation:

Take one-third off the taxable value because the car is over four years old.

Then make the second reduction because you do more than 18,000 business miles

It does not matter in which order you do the calculation – if you reduce by two-thirds and then one-third or by one-third and then two-thirds the answer will be the same.

Tax tip: If possible try to drive at least 2500 business miles a year to save on tax. If your car is to be renewed consider one with a cheaper taxable value or not renewing the car at all as those over four years old have a one-third reduction in the taxable value.

Free fuel from your company
If your company gives you expenses for petrol or diesel for private use of your car, you must declare this under fuel benefits. You do not pay tax if fuel is only provided for business journeys. The tax depends on the engine size of your car. Table 4.3 is for the April 1996 to April 1997 tax year. Remember, you pay tax on the cash equivalent – the cash equivalent is not the amount of tax you pay.

Table 4.3 *Fuel benefits: cash equivalent*

	Cash equivalent for:	
Engine size	Petrol	Diesel
1400cc or less	£710	£640
1401–2000cc	£890	£640
Over 2000cc	£1320	£820

If you make a contribution for fuel for private use, your contributions will **not** reduce the cash equivalent or amount of tax you pay **unless** you reimburse the whole cost of the petrol.

> **Tax tip:** If you rarely use your car for private journeys consider paying your employer for the full cost of this private mileage. That way you escape the fuel benefit tax. You will only gain if you pay more in tax than you receive in free petrol.

1.18: Vans

This covers those who have a van made available to them for private use. Again your employer should have given you details – the cash equivalents are at a fixed rate. If the van was registered on or after 6 April 1993 the cash equivalent is £500. Otherwise it is £350. If you pay your employer for private use of the van, deduct the amount you pay from the cash equivalent. If the van was not exclusively yours for the whole year, reduce the cash value proportionately – so if the van was exclusively yours for only six months you only pay half.

1.19: Interest free and low interest loans

You do not have to include season ticket loans and other loans if the total balance of these is £5000 or less. If the loan is above this you will be taxed on the **total** loan. The amount you are taxed will be the difference between what the loan would have cost you if you had to take the loan from a lender and the actual amount you pay in interest.

The official rate of interest is used in these calculations. Subsidised mortgages may qualify for tax relief. See section 15 of your main Tax Return.

1.20: Mobile phones

As with cars you only have to fill in this box if the phone is available to you for **private use**. If you pay your employer for the full cost of private calls on your mobile phone you **do not** have to pay tax. Otherwise, the cash equivalent is £200 for every phone.

1.21: Private medical or dental insurance

The figure generally is what the actual insurance costs your employer less any contributions you make.

1.22: Other benefits

This covers the total cash equivalent of any other benefits that are not covered in the other boxes. These could include things like:

❑ a chauffeur;
❑ any relocation expenses above £8000 that are not tax free;
❑ nursery place vouchers;
❑ Income Tax paid but not deducted (directors only); and
❑ other assets or services given to you for your private use.

Copy the figures from your P11D.

Some share benefits – for example if your employer enables you to sell shares for more than their market value – should be listed in box **1.22**. If so, they should be listed on your P11D. Otherwise most share benefits should be included in the pages for share schemes.

1.23: Expenses payments received and balancing charges

As this is the final box on benefits you may not think it is important. But all employees who have **expense accounts** or get expenses for things like entertainment or travelling **may** have to fill it in.

If your employer has a dispensation for 1996 to 1997 you may not have to fill in any of the expenses boxes (1.23 as well as **1.32–1.35).**

See *dispensation* explanation earlier in this chapter on page 40. If your employer has a dispensation, you should not have any of these figures on your P11D unless they are expenses that are taxable such as if your employer pays for your home telephone bill.

If your employer does **not** have a dispensation you will have to fill in the box – in this case all expenses should be listed on your P11D. If you want to work out the figures yourself you may need a separate sheet of paper to write down the amount of each type of expense or use the form on page E6 of *How to Fill in Your Tax Return* (the leaflet that comes with your Tax Return). You may also need to add up figures if you have more than one type of expense to write in each box.

❑ *Travelling and subsistence payments*. This will include fares, hotels, meals (you can claim these back in box **1.32**) and travel between home and your normal place of work. *Do not* include any expenses or payments for company car or van expenses or expenses for running your own car if you use it for company business.

❑ *Entertainment*. Put in the total amount you receive – this includes any allowances specifically for entertaining.

❑ *General expenses allowances*. Again, put in the amount of the allowance. So if you get a set allowance for expenses regardless of what you spend on company business you will need to include this.

Remember, if any of these expenses were necessary for your work and were incurred solely in doing your work, you can claim them back as a deduction in boxes **1.32** to **1.35**.

Balancing charges are to tax you for money you have previously claimed as a *capital allowance*. See box **1.35** below for details on how this is calculated.

LUMP SUMS AND COMPENSATION PAYMENTS: BOXES 1.24 TO 1.30

Reliefs are tax free lump sums (one-off cash payments) or the part of a lump sum that is tax free.

1.24 and 1.27: £30,000 exemption

When you are made *redundant*, the first £30,000 of payment you receive is tax free (provided it meets certain criteria) and anything over this is taxed in the normal way through PAYE. Redundancy will include redundancy payments under an Inland Revenue approved or Government scheme, pay in lieu of notice and other payments provided they are not for work done.

When you are made redundant normal wages, pay in lieu of holiday, pay for working your notice period and commission are usually taxed as usual under PAYE and are not tax free. Lump sums that you received in the April 1996 to April 1997 tax year that related to a termination of employment **before** the tax year do not have to be included (you should tell your tax office as these should be included in your tax calculation for the earlier year).

Certain redundancy payments are **not** tax free:

- ❑ Payments made as a term of condition of your employment (it is written into your contract that you will receive a certain pay-off).
- ❑ Payments for work already done.
- ❑ Payments for undertakings not to take another job ('golden hand-cuffs' or restrictive covenants).

Enter in box **1.24** the total amount of redundancy that is tax free. If you received **more** than £30,000, put the figure £30,000 in this box. If you received less, put the amount of qualifying redundancy you received.

Then in box **1.27** put the amount of redundancy received over the £30,000 threshold and any redundancy payments that are taxable.

1.25: Foreign service and disability

Only include the payments, or the part of the payment, that is tax free.

Foreign service covers payments made to you when you were made redundant or received compensation for loss of a job entirely or substantially outside the UK (these are tax free if 75 per cent of your total service was foreign service or the last 10 years out of 20 were foreign service or in a total service of more than 20 years, 50 per cent was foreign). You can claim a partial exemption for some foreign service that does not meet these requirements. See Help Sheet IR204.

Disability covers payments made to you if you could no longer do your job because of injury or disability (accidents are covered in the next box). This payment is tax free.

1.26 and 1.28: Retirement and death lump sums

This box only covers payments from or payments into unapproved retirement benefit schemes. **Your company pension is normally 'approved' so you will not have to worry about filling in this box**. Money your employer pays into a retirement benefit scheme or uses to buy you an annuity (under certain conditions) and certain lump sums from your employer's pension scheme are also tax free. An annuity is an investment scheme usually bought on retirement with the proceeds of your pension fund. It provides you with an income for life.

A few pension schemes are non-approved by the Inland Revenue, these are often 'top-up' schemes for executives who want to boost their pension but have exceeded limits they are allowed to pay into their approved company pension scheme. Some payments from non-approved pension schemes are tax free and do not have to be included in box **1.28**. They are:

❑ Payment on retirement or death as a result of accident;
❑ If the lump sum was funded by contributions you made (you have paid tax on these already);
❑ Or funded by contributions from your employer on which you have already paid tax (these schemes are known as funded unapproved retirement benefit schemes or FURBs).

1.29: Taxable lump sums

You should have already filled in boxes **1.27** and **1.28**. In box **1.29** put remaining lump sums that are taxable including payments for the termination of foreign service that are not exempt or only partially exempt.

1.30: Tax deducted

Write the amount of tax deducted already from items listed in boxes **1.27** to **1.29**. So if you have been made redundant the payment over £30,000 will normally have been taxed already under PAYE – enter the tax deducted or you will pay it twice.

1.31: Foreign earnings not taxable in the UK

You will normally only have to fill in this box if you ticked the non-residence box on page 2 of your core Tax Return. Notes on page E6 of your *Tax Return Guide* explain this in more detail. This box is important as the figure you enter will be deducted from your income before it is taxed (ie it will reduce your tax bill).

HOW TO MAKE SURE THAT YOU ARE NOT TAXED ON EXPENSES: BOXES 1.32–1.36

You **do not have to fill these in if your employer has a dispensation**. You will know if there is **no** dispensation as the full amount of expenses you received will be included on form P11D and you would not normally have filled in box **1.23**.

These boxes allow you to claim back expenses listed in box **1.23**. The reason why you have to fill in these boxes is to make sure you are not taxed on legitimate business expenses as a perk.

If you use your own car for business you should fill in this section to claim back the costs of running your car.

You can **only** list expenses that are necessary travelling expenses and related meal and accommodation costs **incurred in doing your job** and other **necessary** expenses incurred **solely** in doing your job. They must either have been included as expenses received in box **1.23** or have been paid by you but **not** claimed back from your employer.

If you have more than one item to include in this box you will have to add up the total.

1.32: Travel and subsistence costs

You can include business journeys but not journeys to and from your normal place of work. You will be able to claim expenses for journeys to a temporary place of work (see notes on page E7 of the guide on how to fill in your Tax Return). If you are a travelling salesperson or travel as an integral part of your job you can claim the costs incurred from the point you left home. You can also claim for meals while you are on a business journey. You can claim back incidental expenses of £5 for every night spent away from home (newspapers, telephone calls home, etc) but **no** other personal expenses.

If your employer pays certain costs for repairing, insuring and taxing your *company car* direct (ie you do not pay the costs and reclaim them on expenses) it does not affect your tax position. However, if you reclaim these costs on expenses – and these expenses are listed in box **1.23** – you can reclaim the proportion attributable to your business mileage in box **1.32**.

Fill in this box if your mileage allowance is less than the amount which you are allowed to claim without paying tax. See Table 4.1 and text following on page 46 for an explanation of how to calculate this figure.

If you make a claim for mileage allowance in this box you will **not** be able to claim a *capital allowance* to help cover the costs of buying your car (see box **1.35**). You can only claim one or the other.

1.33: Fixed deductions

You should be aware of these as they are agreements made by your Trade Union or worker representative body agreeing a fixed amount for those costs those in your type of work incur. This could be for replacing tools or buying special working clothes. If you want to claim these costs but not under a fixed deduction (for instance, if your costs are higher than agreed) include the costs in box **1.35**.

1.34: Professional fees and subscriptions

These are tax deductible if you have to join a professional body in order to carry out your profession. Ask your professional body for advice on whether your subscriptions are allowable and how much you can deduct.

1.35: Other expenses and capital allowances

Claim any expenses you incurred **necessarily** and **solely** in doing your work. Necessary means the costs everyone doing your job would have to meet and which are unavoidable in doing your job. Also include the business proportion of benefits included in full in box **1.22**, director's and employee's liability insurance, the cost of upkeep of tools and special clothing and any other expense not covered in boxes **1.32** to **1.34**.

The *capital allowances* you can claim are for the cost of equipment or machinery you use or have to provide for carrying out your job. Generally you can only claim for items necessary for you to carry out your duties – for example office equipment – but you can also include **private cars used for business** provided you have **not** already claimed for running costs under the mileage allowance (although you can claim the business proportion of running costs in box 1.32).

To qualify for a capital allowance, the items must have a useful life of at least two years and must be things which every person doing your job would have to provide. However, the most common item to come into this category is a private car used for business. If you have bought any other equipment ask for Help Sheet IR203.

The *capital allowance* you can deduct on cars is 25 per cent of the cost of the car; and in subsequent years a further 25 per cent of the balance.

So, if the car costs £12,000
Year 1 capital allowance is 25 per cent of £12,000 = **£3000** (put this figure in box **1.35**)

Year 2 you can claim a capital allowance on the remaining balance
£12,000 – £3000 (which you have already claimed) = **£9000** (the written down value)
Year 2 capital allowance is 25 per cent of £9000 = **£2250**

This writing down continues until the car is worthless, sold or you no longer use it for business. The maximum allowance in a year is £3000. You can only claim the proportion attributed to business. So if 1000 of your 10,000 total miles were on business, you can only claim one-tenth of the purchase price as a capital allowance. This is known as the *business proportion*. You will have to keep detailed records of mileage to prove this. When you sell the car if the amount you sell it for exceeds the written down value you will have to pay tax on the difference. This is known as a *balancing charge* and it is taxed in box **1.23**.

Tax tip: You can also get tax relief on interest paid on loans you take out to buy a car which you use in your employer's business and on which you can claim capital allowances. The interest relief can be claimed in the first four years of the loan. Again relief is restricted to business use of the vehicle. You should claim this in box **1.32** along with other running and maintenance costs.

1.36: Travel from home to work

Tick the box if your expenses include money for travel to and from work as this is not allowed as a deductible expense and as such the Inland Revenue will want to know if you have included this in your expenses boxes. If you receive expenses for this travel, you will be taxed on the amount you receive.

1.37: Foreign earnings deduction

Write the amount of earnings you received while working abroad during the 'qualifying period' of 365 days or more (with no single visits of more than 62 consecutive days). This will ensure that you are not taxed on these earnings. Ask for Help Sheet 205. There are special rules for seafarers.

1.38: Foreign tax relief

Only fill this in if you do **not** want to claim back foreign tax you have paid on your employment income. If you **do** want to claim tax relief you must include the amount of tax you are claiming on the Foreign pages. See Chapter 7 in this section.

Important: If you have – or had during the tax year – more than one job or employment you must fill in a separate Employment form for each job.

If you did not tick any other boxes on page 2 of your Tax Return you can now go back to *step 2* and tick the box that states that you have filled in your supplementary pages. Then turn straight to Chapter 11 for details on how to fill in the rest of your Tax Return.

3

SHARE SCHEMES

Only fill in these pages if you ticked the Share Scheme box on page 2 of your core Tax Return.

> **Important:** These pages only cover Income Tax due – Capital Gains Tax (the profit you make when you sell shares) is covered on a separate page. Profits on the sale of shares are taxable because once you own the shares they are no longer in the tax free scheme.

Dividends from shares received through an employee share scheme (the dividends you earn after you have converted your savings into shares) should **not** be included here. Include them on page 3 of your Tax Return.

Many share schemes are tax exempt – so you may not have to fill in any of the boxes even though you received shares from a share scheme during the tax year.

The following should not be included in the Share Scheme pages:

❑ **Approved* profit sharing scheme**. If you are in an **approved profit sharing scheme** – a scheme which gives a yearly tax free allocation of shares to employees – shares are only taxed if they are kept in the Scheme Trust less than three years (five years for periods up to 28 April 1996).

If these shares are taxable, PAYE will normally have already been deducted. Your employer or the trustees of the profit sharing scheme will tell you how much has been paid to you and how much tax has been deducted so you can include the figures in your employee payments box **1.10** and your employee tax deducted box **1.11** on your Employment form.

❑ **Save-As-You-Earn (SAYE) scheme**. If you are in a **Save-As-You-Earn (SAYE) scheme** – also known as an 'approved savings-related share option scheme' – run by your employer you will have been offered the chance to buy shares at a discount. This is a share option. The shares can be purchased at discount of up to 20 per cent lower than the stock market value on the date your option is granted. You can save up to £250 a month to buy these shares and after five or seven years buy the shares (depending on the scheme contract) or take your savings. The only tax you may have to pay is Capital Gains Tax when you sell the shares.

These schemes are tax free and you **do not** have to fill in these pages provided:

    – you have **not** taken your shares *(exercised your option)* within three years of being granted the share option; and
    – **not** bought your shares within three years because your company was taken over; and
    – your scheme is approved by the Inland Revenue.

❑ **Approved executive share option scheme**. If you are in an **approved executive share option scheme** also known as a 'discretionary share options scheme' and were granted the options before 17 July 1995 you **do not** have to pay tax or fill in these pages provided:

---

*   Note: 'approved' means approved as a tax free scheme by the Inland Revenue.

- the scheme is approved; and
- the option is exercised within three and ten years; and
- at least three years after any previous options were exercised (this can be under any approved discretionary share option scheme for which Income Tax relief was given, for instance another, or the same, executive share option scheme); and

If the share option was granted to you after 17 July 1995 the gain is **not** taxable unless the total value of all shares granted to you (subject to approved options) is more than £30,000 at the time the new options are granted.

If you are in an unapproved scheme you will pay Income Tax on the difference between the *market value* when you buy your shares (exercise the option) and the amount (if any) you paid for the option. The market value is not the stockmarket closing price but an agreed value between your employer and the Shares Valuation Division of the Inland Revenue. Ask your employer if you are uncertain of the value to use.

PAPERWORK REQUIRED

You will need a separate page S2 (the second page) for each Share Scheme *'event'* that is taxable. An *event* is every time you *exercised an option* (bought shares) or an option was *granted* (you were given the option to buy shares at a later date).

You will need to have your share option certificate, copy of any exercise notice, any correspondence or other explanatory information received from your employer about the share transaction and information on the market value of the shares at the relevant dates.

If your Share Scheme 'event' is taxable, you should also have the Inland Revenue notes on Share Schemes.

Before you can fill in the form you need to know if the shares were *unquoted* – this simply means they were not quoted (or listed) on the Stock Exchange or the Unlisted Securities Market (USM). Tick the unquoted boxes if the shares were not listed on the Stock Exchange.

SHARE OPTIONS

Share options are schemes giving employees an *option* to buy shares in the company for which they work at a favourable price at a later date.

Page S1 only has to be filled in once – regardless of how many share options you exercise. If you have shares in more than one company, list one name in box **2.1** and the other in the 'Additional information' box at the bottom of the page.

APPROVED SAVINGS-RELATED SHARE OPTIONS: BOXES 2.1–2.6

You probably know these as *Save-As-You-Earn* schemes. However, you **only** have to fill this in if the share options are taxable (the criteria are explained at the beginning of this chapter).

To work out the taxable value fill in boxes **2.32** to **2.41** on page S2. You do not have to fill in box **2.38** if you did not pay for the option (for instance, if you were in an SAYE scheme).

If you have been given money for giving up the option or for not exercising it (for instance when your company was taken over) this is classed as a *cancellation or release* so fill in that column rather than the exercise column. Cancellation or release also covers receiving something for transferring, cancelling, realising or not exercising your option.

Box 2.1

Fill in the name of the company. Tick box **2.2** if the shares are in an unquoted company. If you have filled in this box also fill in boxes **2.32** and **2.33** on page S2 and fill in the boxes in the Exercise column. The date the option was granted was the date you joined the SAYE scheme.

Box 2.3: Taxable amount

This is the market value of the share (put the value per share in box **2.40** on page S2) on the day you bought the shares or exercised the option (put this date in box **2.35**) *less* the price you actually paid for the shares – the option price per share (put this in box **2.37** in the

Exercise column), *multiplied* by the number of shares you bought (put this in box **2.36** in the Exercise column).

So, if the shares were quoted at £2 on the day you exercised your option and you bought them for an option price of only £1.50 then your taxable amount is £2 – £1.50 = 50p per share. Multiply this by the number of shares you bought. So, if you bought 1000, the taxable amount would be 1000 × 50p = £500. Enter this figure in box **2.3**.

Boxes 2.4 and 2.5: Cancellation or release

As described above, this is where you receive money for not exercising your share option or for giving it up. Write in the name of the company (boxes **2.4** and **2.32**). If you have already filled in box **2.32** you will need to request a second share schemes form. But only fill in page 2 of this second form.

Calculate the taxable amount in the same way as in box **2.3** but instead of using the price you bought the shares for use the amount you were paid for not exercising your option. On page S2 fill in the boxes in the cancellation/release column.

APPROVED DISCRETIONARY SHARE OPTIONS

These are often restricted to middle and senior management and are known as executive share option schemes. You will not have to fill in these boxes if your Share Scheme met the criteria listed at the beginning of this chapter.

If your options are taxable, you will pay tax on the difference between the market value of the shares at the time you exercised the option and the amount paid for the shares.

Boxes **2.10–2.12** should be filled in in the same way as boxes **2.4** to **2.6**.

UNAPPROVED SHARE OPTIONS

Unapproved share options may be taxed on **both** the grant (or giving) of the share option **and** the exercise (or taking) of a share option.

Boxes 2.13–2.15: Grant

This covers tax you may have to pay when the option is granted to you. Only fill this in if the option price is less than the market value of the shares at the date the option was granted to you **or** if you can buy the shares (exercise the option) in an unapproved scheme more than seven years after the option was granted to you.

Fill in the *grant* column on page S2 and include any amount you had to pay when you took out the option in box **2.38**.

The value of the option (a **minimum** of the share's market value or higher if it is worth more) **less** the price you paid for the option (if any) is the amount that is taxable.

Boxes 2.16–2.18: Exercise

This applies when you exercise the option. You only have to include unapproved schemes (**not** approved ones where the option price of the shares is lower than the market value).

Boxes 2.19 and 2.21: Cancellation or release

Read the notes above for boxes **2.4** and **2.5** for an explanation of how this works. The taxable amount you enter into box **2.21** is the amount you receive for cancelling or releasing options less the amount you paid for the option in the first place.

SHARES AS EMPLOYEE BENEFITS

Shares you get as a result of your employment are treated as an employee benefit for tax purposes. You need to fill in the shares acquired section if, because of your employment, you were able to buy shares or an interest in shares for **less** than they were worth at the time or you were given them for **free**.

Boxes 2.22–2.24: Shares received from your employment

The taxable amount is calculated as follows:

1. Take the market value of the shares (put this in box **2.47** in the column shares acquired) and **multiply** this by the number of shares (put this in box **2.45** under the shares acquired column).
2. **Deduct** the amount you paid per share (put this in box **2.46**) **multiplied by** the number of shares you bought.
3. This gives you the taxable amount (put this in box **2.24**).

Boxes 2.25–2.27: Shares as a benefit

The difference between this box and the one above is that it covers shares that you can buy cheaply because of your job – not because the company was offering the shares to its employees.

Instead of being taxed on the saving as you are in boxes **2.22–2.27** you are taxed as though you received an interest free loan to buy the shares. This also covers shares you buy in instalments. So if you buy shares worth £10,000 and pay only £2500, you are taxed as though you were given an interest free loan for the difference £10,000 – £2500 = £7500. You are taxed on the interest you would have paid to take out a loan to pay for the remaining £7500 of shares. Tax is on interest at the official rate. When you sell the shares you pay back the 'loan' – say £7500 – by entering it as a taxable amount in box **2.27**.

So if you bought the shares at the beginning of the tax year you

> **T**ax tip: If you have bought shares in a close company which has a closed or limited number of shareholders, and you were a shareholder with a stake of more than 5 per cent or worked in running the business you can claim tax relief on interest paid on actual loans to buy shares. The same applies if you buy shares in an employee-controlled company. See Help Sheet IR216.

Box 2.28: Post-acquisition charges

This taxes you for the increased value of the shares bought in your company under the 'Shares received from your employment' and 'Shares as benefits' sections and also for any benefits you received because you owned the shares (such as dividends). See Help Sheet IR217 for a full explanation and how to work out the figures.

4

SELF-EMPLOYMENT

The self-employed face two major tax changes this year – Self Assessment and the change to *current year* accounting. **You should understand the implications of both of these**. If you do not you could fill in your Tax Return incorrectly. By making the most of the changes you could **cut the tax payable over two years in half**.

This chapter is aimed primarily at the self-employed who do not have an accountant, who want to know what information to give their accountant or tax agent and who want a better understanding of how they are taxed and what they can deduct to reduce their overall tax bill.

This form must be filled in by anyone who was self-employed at any time during the 6 April 1996 to 5 April 1997 tax year.

You must be a sole trader – running a business on your own and responsible for its debts and liabilities. If you are running the business with someone else – in **partnership** – these details should be included on the Partnership pages. Companies are taxed under a different system and pay Corporation Tax. Income earned as an employee or company director must be included in the **Employment** pages as this is not classed as self-employment. Dividends from companies that are not connected with your business and any **investment income** such as bank interest that is **not** part of your trading income should be included on your main Tax Return in the sections covering shares and bank and building society interest. **Rents** should be included under Land and Property unless you rent out land or property as part of your business.

The Inland Revenue has special rules to help those whose profits are irregular and who may have self-employed earnings one year and none the next. If you are an author or artist, a farmer or market gardener or a foster carer or adult carer, ask the Inland Revenue for the special rules that will help you to even out your tax bill.

If your turnover is small (less than £15,000 a year) and you do not have a balance sheet (the document that lists your assets and liabilities), the amount of information you will be required to provide will be greatly reduced. However, all self-employed people may have to do additional calculations on separate pieces of paper, so there will be more work to do than just filling your tax return.

PAPERWORK REQUIRED

One copy of the Self-employment pages for each set of business accounts (unless your turnover is less than £15,000). These are the accounts drawn up at the end of the tax year. Because two years of accounts (1995 to 1996 and 1996 to 1997) may have to be included on the 1996 to 1997 Tax Return you may have two sets and as such will require a second self-employment form. You will also have more than one set of accounts if you run more than one business. If you do not have accounts drawn up, you will need records of income and expenditure.

You will need the guidance notes on self-employment from the Inland Revenue and any Help Sheets (listed at the front of the guidance notes) and any tax leaflets relevant to your business. If you have not got these ask for them by telephoning the Orderline on 0645 000 404.

If you pay tax 'on account' (in two instalments) you should have been sent a 'Self Assessment – Statement of Account' form – a tax bill sent for payment by 31 January 1997. You will need this, and the notice of the second instalment in July, to calculate how much tax you still owe for the 1996 to 1997 tax year.

Tax payment dates: These have changed from 1 January and 1 July to 31 January and 31 July.

WHAT IF I ONLY RECEIVE OCCASIONAL, SMALL OR PART-TIME EARNINGS?

If you are an employee who earns extra money from freelance or consultancy work this is classed as self-employment. Remember, you can be an employee **and** self-employed. And you can be self-employed on a part-time or spare-time basis. Although you may not think that you are running your own business, for tax purposes you are. Only if you receive very isolated payments can you avoid filling in the self-employment pages. If this is the case you can put these additional earnings on page 4 of your Tax Return.

If you are unsure as to whether or not you are self-employed you must generally:

❑ work for more than one person or employer;
❑ pick the hours you work;
❑ provide your own tools and equipment;
❑ operate your own business structure – invoicing, opening a business bank account, etc;
❑ determine what work you do and how you carry it out;
❑ take financial risks – investing your own money in your business.

The 'badges of trade' which determine whether or not you are investing (or doing something as a hobby) or trading are:

❑ **Frequency or number of similar transactions by the same person.** You buy and sell similar items with the aim of making a profit and do so frequently – for instance, you buy and sell a lot of antiques.
❑ **Buying and selling within a short period of time**. If you sell items which you have not owned for very long.
❑ **Supplementary work**. If you alter or improve items so you can make more when you sell them – for instance, you restore classic cars and then sell them on for a profit on a frequent basis. Supplementary work also includes money spent on advertising.
❑ **Motive**. If your motive for buying and selling is to make a profit.
❑ **Subject matter of the sale**. If you sell something that you bought for your own use or benefit then you are not trading. But if you sell things that you bought with the aim of making a profit you could be classed as self-employed.

THE CHANGE TO CURRENT YEAR ACCOUNTING

Instead of being taxed on the *preceding year's* profits, businesses will now be taxed on the *current year's* profits. In the past the self-employed who set up business before 6 April 1994 included on their Tax Return their profits for their accounting year ending in the tax year before. For example, on the April 1995 to April 1996 Tax Return you would have included profits for the accounting year ending in the preceding tax year – any time between April 1994 and April 1995.

This meant that if the accounting year ended on 5 May 1994 these profit details were not declared until the Tax Return arrived in April 1996 and this did not have to be filled in and returned until 31 October 1996. Tax was paid in instalments on 1 January 1996 and 1 July with any final tax payments at the end of the year giving a considerable time lag between earning profits and paying tax on them.

From the April 1997 to April 1998 tax year, all self-employed will be taxed on a current year's basis and will have to give details of their profits in the *accounting year* ending in the *tax year*. So if your account-ing year ends on 5 May 1997 you will include profits for the 12 months to 5 May 1997 on your 1997/1998 Tax Return – and then pay this tax on the new payment dates of 31 January 1998 and 31 July 1998 (for payments on account) and the final balancing payment by 31 January 1999. So the new current year system means you have to pay tax much sooner after you earn your profits.

The 1995 to 1996 tax year was the last one in which you were taxed on the preceding year basis.

So during the *transitional year* 1996 to 1997 you will need to catch up – you will have to produce accounts for the *preceding* year (1995 to 1996) **and** the *current* year (1996 to 1997). These will be the 12-month accounting periods that ended in each of those tax years. So this could be the year to 31 December 1995 and the year to 31 December 1996 or whenever your accounting year ends.

Instead of charging you for the preceding year's tax **and** the current year's tax in one year – which would mean paying twice as much tax as normal – the Inland Revenue will charge half the tax owed for the two years.

You will save more tax if you make more profits in these two years. As any expenses deductions you make against tax will effectively be halved (along with your profits) it will pay you to make deductions in later tax years. However, you can still claim the full amount of losses against your tax (these will not be halved during the *transitional years* while tax is being switched from preceding to current year).

> **T**ax tip: If you want to boost the amount of profits that are included in the transitional period you can do so by changing your accounting year. But you can only bring your accounting date **closer to** 5 April 1997.

The change will not affect every business and some will make greater savings than others.

Who will not be affected

Businesses set up **after 5 April 1994** are already taxed on a *current year basis*. The date you started to 'trade' is the date you started in business (not necessarily the date you first received payment).

Who will be affected

Businesses set up **on or before 5 April 1994**. However, some of those with small amounts of, or occasional, self-employed earnings who set up in business before 4 April 1994 may already be on a current year accounting basis. For these businesses it is known as *actual year* accounting. If you filled in your self-employed income for the year to 5 April 1996 on your 1995/1996 Tax Return you are already taxed on a current year basis.

THE BASIS PERIOD RULES

To fill this in you need to know your *accounting year* – the 12 month period over which you calculate your profits – and your *accounting date*, the date on which that period ends.

BUSINESSES SET UP ON OR AFTER 6 APRIL 1994

When it comes to working out your profits on your Tax Return you will have to calculate them over your *basis period*.

This basis period may or may not be the same as your accounting period and although it will usually be a 12-month period it may be longer or shorter.

If you set up in business between 6 April 1994 and 5 April 1995 your basis period will be the 12 months to your accounting date in the 1996 to 1997 tax year. So if your accounting year ran from 6 April 1996 to 5 April 1997, this will be your basis period.

If you set up in business between 6 April 1995 and 5 April 1996 then your basis period will be:

❑ *either* the first 12 months of trading;

❑ *or*, if your accounting date is **more than 12 months** after the date on which you started in business, the 12 months to your accounting date (the date you have chosen as the end of your accounting year). The accounting date must be within the tax year 6 April 1996 to 5 April 1997;

❑ *or*, if your accounting date is **less than 12 months** after the date on which you started in business, your basis period will be the 12 months beginning on the date you set up in business.

If you started in business after 6 April 1994 and you ceased trading in the period from 6 April 1996 to 5 April 1997, your basis period will be up to the date your business ceased. The basis period start date will be the day after your accounting year end in the 1995 to 1996 tax year. So if your accounting year ends on 6 May then the start date for your basis period will be 7 May 1995. You may have a basis period of longer than 12 months.

If you closed a business you should read the section on overlap profits later in this chapter.

If you have changed your accounting date you should read Help Sheet IR222 to see how to calculate your basis period.

BUSINESSES SET UP BEFORE 6 APRIL 1994

If you started in business before 6 April 1994 and you sold or closed down your business before 6 April 1997 your basis period for 1996 to 1997 is the period 6 April 1996 to the date you ceased in business. You do **not** need to switch from a preceding year to a current year basis.

If you made a loss in your last year of trading and your business ceased in the 1996 to 1997 tax year, you can offset the loss of the final 12 months trading against any profits from the same business which were taxed in the 1993/1994 to 1995/1996 tax years. This will reduce your tax bill retrospectively so you may get a tax rebate.

If you started in business before 6 April 1994 and you were still in business on 6 April 1997, your basis period will cover two accounting years.

Your basis period will **start** the day after the end of the last period for which you were assessed for tax. That would have been included on your 1995/1996 Tax Return. But remember you used to be taxed on a preceding year's basis. So if your business year ends on 30 June, the year 30 June 1994 would have been the last period for which you were assessed for tax. So your starting date for the basis period is the day after (you have already been assessed on profits up to 30 June). So it will be 1 July 1994.

Your basis period will **end** on your accounting date which falls in the 1996 to 1997 tax year. If your accounting dates have not changed your basis period will be 24 months. To continue with the example above, this will be 30 June 1996. **You will have to provide accounts for both of the years in your basis period, but you only have to work out your average profits once.**

To average your profits over 12 months you take the profits made in the basis period and multiply them by $^{12}/_{24}$ or $^{1}/_{2}$.

If you have changed accounting dates your basis period may be more than 24 months. So if the basis period was 30 months you would multiply your basis period profits by $^{12}/_{30}$.

By extending your accounting year to cover more profits, you actually cut the amount of tax you pay on these profits.

Tax tip: Although the examples here use a fraction (say 12/24 = ½% × profits) to calculate the average profits over 12 months, 1996 was a leap year so it may be more accurate to use what the Inland Revenue calls an 'appropriate fraction'. Instead of using months, calculate the average in days using 365/the number of days in the two accounting periods. So if you have a 24-month period the fraction will be 365/(365 + 366) = 0.499% of profits.

OVERLAP PROFITS AND CHANGING YOUR ACCOUNTING YEAR

If you have changed accounting year some of your profits may be taxed twice. For example, if your new accounting date in 1996–1997 is **less** than 12 months after your last accounting date it will cover some of the profits that have already been taxed. If your last taxed period was to 31 December 1995 and your new accounting date is 31 September, your basis period will be the 12 months from 1 October 1995 to 31 September 1996. But this means that profits in the period between 1 October 1995 and 31 December 1995 will overlap and will be **taxed twice**.

As you will be taxed twice at a time when most businesses are getting tax on their profits halved, you can claim *overlap relief* on these *overlap profits*. This will reduce your tax bill. Put the amount in box **3.78** on page SE3 of your Self-employment form.

To calculate the relief **divide** the number of overlap days (say 62 if the overlap is from 1 October to 31 December) **by** 366 (the number of days in this year as it was a leap year) and then **multiply** this by the profits in the 12 months of your basis period (your last accounting year).

IF YOU DO NOT HAVE ACCOUNTS DRAWN UP

You no longer need to send your statement of accounts in with your Tax Return. However, you will still need to have accounts to fill in your Tax Return. If you are running a substantial business, it may pay you to employ an accountant – **accountancy fees are tax deductible**. However, you can draw up your own accounts if your turnover is low, you do not employ a large staff and you know what is required – your accounts must meet accepted accountancy standards. If you are unsure how these work, ask your Tax Office for advice and for Help Sheets IR225 and IR229.

Remember, your turnover should include the value of sales you have made in the accounting year including invoices you have sent out for services provided – even if you have not yet been paid.

You do not need to have a balance sheet to fill in your Tax Return but if your business involves keeping stocks you may find this useful.

IF YOUR BUSINESS MAKES A LOSS

You can offset losses to reduce your tax liability in either the same year as you made the loss or in other accounting years.

You can claim tax relief for your losses by making a deduction from:

❑ Your total income for the year (but include this in the Self-employment pages). This includes investment income and **earnings from employment**.

❑ As a deduction from your capital gains (include your figure in the Capital Gains pages).

❑ By reducing your business profits taxed in earlier years if you have now ceased to trade.

❑ Or by carrying forward your losses to offset against future profits.

Although profits will be halved in most cases over the two-year transitional period, losses will not. So you can still get **full relief for losses made in the transitional period**. If you have made a loss and your business was set up before 6 April 1994 ask for Help Sheet IR230 and IR227.

Tax tip: If you made a loss on one of the two years in your basis period, you do not have to use this loss to reduce profits in the other year. You can carry it forward to set against future profits. This will help you to keep profits as high as possible during the transitional period to make the most of tax reductions.

Tax tip: If you set up in business before 6 April 1994 and have any losses that you have brought forward (you have not yet used to reduce profits), you should avoid using them to reduce profits in the basis period. Profits (and therefore tax) will be halved so you will want to have the highest profits possible.

Tax tip: If you want to offset losses against other income in the transitional 1996 to 1997 tax year ask your tax office for advice on how much you can claim.

Tax tip: If you have made a loss during the first four tax years of your business, you can set this loss against other income including earnings from a job. You can offset the loss against money you earned in the three tax years before the year in which the loss was made. *So you could get a tax rebate on the tax you have paid on your salary.* To get this relief you must show that you will make a profit within a reasonable period.

WHAT YOU CAN DEDUCT TO REDUCE YOUR TAX BILL

Generally you can deduct any expense that is incurred *wholly and exclusively* for the purpose of the business you run. Employees must also show that these expenses are *necessarily* incurred. So as a self-employed person you have more freedom to deduct expenses from your income to reduce your profits – and in turn your tax bill. You do not have to prove that expenses were necessary and even the 'wholly and exclusively' rule has exceptions – you can claim for your car if you use it for both personal and business use but only the proportion of costs that relate to business use.

This makes expenses easier to justify. Basically you can **deduct most expenses and expenditure which forms part of your day-to-day running costs, apart from:**

❑ anything you buy for personal or domestic use;
❑ most entertainment expenses;
❑ capital items such as business premises, equipment and any expenditure incurred with such items, for example the legal expense of acquiring them (these capital items are tax deductible – but under capital allowances); and
❑ your own wages.

If an item is not used wholly and exclusively you can only claim a proportion of it against tax – the portion you use for business. For instance, you may use your car for both business and private purposes. So you will only be able to claim the proportion of car expenses which is attributable to business use. You can work this out on a mileage basis. So if half your mileage is for business you should be able to deduct half your car expenses.

The Inland Revenue provides a list of what you can and cannot deduct on page 4 of Help Sheet IR255 – ask for this if you have not received it.

WHAT CAN BE CLAIMED AS A CAPITAL ALLOWANCE

Major purchases are **not** deducted as business expenses. If you buy a computer or machinery this is not an *allowable business expense*. It is classed as a capital expenditure and as such it should be deducted as a *capital allowance*.

Capital allowances are given on items of equipment or capital assets:

❑ Plant and machinery – including machines and computers, furniture, ladders and scaffolding, tools and equipment, vans and lorries (include computer software only if you buy this as part of your computer package). You can write these off at 25 per cent a year.
❑ Cars (25 per cent).
❑ Industrial buildings – if you run a factory, but not if you run a shop (4 per cent).
❑ Fixtures and fittings (25 per cent).

You can only get capital allowances on items used *wholly and exclusively* for the business and that belong to the business. But you can claim a proportion of the costs of cars that are for part business and part private use.

Capital allowances cover those items that have a useful life of more than two or three years. So buying computer software may be an allowable business expense (100 per cent tax deductible) rather than a capital allowance (unless you buy the software as a package with your computer).

Tax tip: If you spent money on setting up your business before you actually started trading you can also claim pre-trading expenses. So money you spend on rent and rates or business equipment while setting up your business can be tax deducted. The expenses can be incurred up to seven years before your business actually starts. But you claim this under *loss relief* **not** under expenses or capital allowances.

Tax tip: If you buy equipment for private use (such as a computer) and then use it in your business, you can claim a capital allowance on its market value at the time you start using it for business.

Tax tip: If you buy on hire purchase, you can claim capital allowances on the original cost of the item (the part you pay). The extra amount you pay in interest or other charges can be claimed as a business expense.

HOW TO WORK OUT YOUR CAPITAL ALLOWANCES

For plant and machinery – computers, etc – you can claim up to **25 per cent** of the cost in the year in which you buy it. The rest is written off over a number of years at up to 25 per cent of the remaining value. For example:

You spend **£3000** on a computer:

In the year you bought it you can deduct 25 per cent as a capital allowance =
£750
It now has a *written down* value of £3,000 – £750 = **£2250**

In the second year you can claim a capital allowance of 25 per cent on this
written down value of £2250
25 per cent of £2250 = **£562.50**
The written down value is now £2250 – £562.50 = **£1687.50**

You continue writing down your capital until it is completely written off, you
sell the items or they are no longer being used for business purposes.

To make things more simple, items may be grouped together and treated as a *pool of expenditure* so that you do not have to calculate each item separately. You take the written down value of all items in each pool (these are listed on your Tax Return) and deduct 25 per cent (or the rate that applies to that pool).

Cars, but not lorries and vans, must be calculated separately or in their own pool if you have purchased more than one. The maximum you can write down in any year is £3000 on each car. Cars which cost more than £12,000 cannot be included in this pool and must be calculated separately as must **cars used partly for private motoring**.

When you sell your asset, give it away or it ceases to be of any use a separate calculation must be made. The *balancing charge* or *balancing allowance* taxes you for any profit you make from selling an asset for more than the amount you have deducted from your tax bill (the *written down value*). It also compensates you for any losses – if you sell an asset for less than the written down value. If you give an asset away you must calculate this figure using the market value.

So if the written down value was £10,000 and you sold the asset for £7000 you would get a balancing allowance of £3000 and could claim this loss to reduce your tax bill. You write it as a negative amount (put it in brackets) in the balancing charge boxes of your Tax Return. If you scrap the asset you deduct the remaining written down value.

But if you sold the asset for £13,000, you would have a balancing charge of £3000 and would pay tax on this as it will be added to your profits.

If you are a new business and your accounting period is not 12 months you must reduce your capital allowances proportionately. So if you have only been in business for six months you can only claim half the capital allowance.

HOW TO FILL IN THE SELF-EMPLOYMENT TAX PAGES

If you want to explain any figures or clarify a point use the Additional information boxes on your Self-employment form. Your notes may answer any questions the tax office may have and save them having to write to you or make an enquiry into your accounts.

This is particularly important this year because the Inland Revenue will be looking out for those trying to abuse the transitional rules for the move from preceding year to current year accounting.

PAGE SE1

Boxes 3.1, 3.2 and 3.3

Enter the name of your business – if you do not have a business name enter your own name, a brief description of your trade (for example builder) and your trading address (or home address if you work from home). Fill in box **3.6** if any of these details have changed.

If you have more than one business you **must** complete boxes **3.1** to **3.3** on a separate set of self-employment pages.

Boxes 3.4–3.5

This is the accounting period for which you are providing details of income and expenses. If you have more than one accounting period and set of accounts in your basis period you will need to fill in an additional form. Do not write your basis period in this box unless it is the same as your accounting period.

Box 3.7

In most cases you should not have to tick this box. Your *basis period* should start on the day after your last accounting date ended. If you are a new business this will be apparent from box **3.9**. However, if you have changed accounting dates, you may have to tick this box.

Box 3.8

You will probably want to tick this box because it tells you to disclose that you have applied the anti-avoidance rules. **Do not**. If you tick it you will be telling the tax office that you **have exploited** the transitional period rules to boost profits and reduce your tax, but that you **will deduct any tax benefit**. By declaring that you have exploited the transitional rules (instead of waiting for the Inland Revenue to find out) you avoid penalties.

The Inland Revenue is prepared for any abuses of the changes in the way the self-employed are taxed and has set up anti-avoidance procedures. You will meet the anti-avoidance rules if you:

❑ **have** followed the basis rules;

❑ **have not** changed your accounting date (other than to bring it closer to 5 April 1997);

❑ **have not** changed your established business practice. If you have a major item of expenditure every year such as an annual maintenance bill and you defer this during the transitional period to maximise profits, this could be considered a change of business practices to reduce your tax bill. Changes that do not affect the timing of expenditure or profits will normally be allowed;

❑ **have not** made any self-cancelling transactions known as 'relevant transactions' – if you have sold something that you intend to buy back after the end of the tax year and the aim of this is to gain a tax advantage it will not be allowed;

❑ if you **have not** entered into a transaction with a connected person (a relative, even distant ones such as grandsons-in-law) or a company that is under common control;

❑ **have not** changed or modified your accounting policy – for instance changing the way you value stock.

Even if you have taken advantage of the tax benefits of the transitional period, you can avoid a penalty provided you only make minimal extra profits or your aim was not to reduce your tax liability.

Boxes 3.9 and 3.10

If the start date of your business is after 5 April 1994, fill in the date in box **3.9**. It will let the Inland Revenue know you are already taxed on a current year basis. But you must still use the correct basis period in your accounts.

If you sold or closed down your business enter the date it ceased and check you are using the correct basis period when you work out your accounts.

Boxes 3.11 to 3.13: Businesses with a turnover below £15,000

If you have a statement of accounts use the figures that are included on that – then fill in the three boxes and go to page SE3.

If your *annual turnover* is less than £15,000 (not your turnover over the basis period, which may be longer than your accounting year) and you have **more than one business** you **must** complete a set of self-employment pages for each business. The £15,000 figure is reduced proportionately if you have been in business for less than a year – so if you have been in business for six months the limit is £7500.

If you only have one business but have more than one set of

accounts covering the basis period you do **not** have to fill in a separate set of self-employment pages for each set of accounts.

Remember to use the accounting years that are included in your basis period – but if your basis period is over 12 months do not average your turnover, expenses and profits over 12 months. The adjustment is made to your profits on page SE3. If your basis period is more than 12 months **it may appear that you have an annual turnover in excess of £15,000.**

Boxes 3.11 and 3.12

Your turnover must include sales and other business receipts and:

❑ include the normal selling price of any goods you have taken for personal use or for your family or friends;

❑ include income which has been earned but not received (see 'If do not have accounts drawn up' earlier in this chapter);

❑ do not include interest from your bank or building society (put that on your main Tax Return with other savings income);

❑ do not include any capital allowances or balancing charges – these cover capital assets such as buildings, machinery, cars, computers. These are included on page SE3.

❑ do not include Enterprise Allowance or Business Start Up Allowance (that goes in box **3.88**)

Box 3.13

Your profit or loss is your income minus your expenses. Write your loss in brackets.

The Tax Return advises you to go straight to page SE3. However, if you have drawn up your own accounts and are worried that you may have left something out, take a photocopy of page SE2 and work through boxes **3.14** to **3.57**.

PAGE SE2

A separate set of income and expenses pages must be filled in if you have more than one business or more than one set of accounts and your turnover is £15,000 or more a year.

Boxes 3.14 and 3.15: VAT

If you are not registered for VAT you can claim back any VAT paid on expenses or equipment. Include VAT in the cost of each item. You do not have to tick boxes **3.14** or **3.15**.

Only tick boxes **3.14** or **3.15** if you are registered for VAT. You can either include VAT in **all** your figures, including income and expenses – or you can exclude it in **all** cases.

If you include VAT write your net payment to Customs and Excise in box **3.50**. If you received a net repayment from Customs and Excise include this in the figure in box **3.37**.

Read page SE4 of the Inland Revenue guidance notes on self-employment for more information.

Boxes 3.16: Turnover

Enter your sales/business income – remember, turnover is all the money earned but not necessarily received (excluding Enterprise Allowance or Business Start up Allowance which go in box **3.38**) before you deduct business expenses.

If your basis period is more than 12 months (more than one accounting period), you must include the turnover of the second accounting period on a second self-employment form **if you have drawn up more than one set of accounts**. Remember you use the basis period calculation only for profits – and only the profits in boxes **3.68** and **3.93** (these must be included only once on one form if you have filled in a second set of self-employment pages).

Income from sales of goods or services is classed as being earned at the time of sale or when you provide them – so even if you do not receive payment for many months, your turnover should include the figures for goods and services provided in the accounting year, **not** just those that were paid for during the accounting year. Even if you have not issued a bill, you earn the income at the time the goods or services are provided.

Turnover includes receipts in cash or in kind for goods sold or work done, commissions, etc. You should also include in your turnover any amounts you have paid for goods taken out of the business for your personal use or for your family and friends (the difference between this price and the normal selling price should go in box **3.54**).

Do not include any capital receipts – this is money you received or the part-exchange value on the sale of capital assets such as machinery or business equipment (this goes in boxes **3.59** to **3.67**).

Boxes 3.17 and 3.33: Cost of sales

This covers the cost of buying raw materials to make your goods or provide your service and stock you buy for resale. This must include items that you have received but not yet paid for. Costs of sales can even include petrol if you are a taxi driver or run a haulage business as you are effectively buying fuel and selling it on. You can only normally claim for the costs of goods and raw materials used to make items actually sold. However, you can deduct the costs of raw materials that are part-way through manufacturing and costs incurred in large service contracts as *work-in-progress* costs. Ask for Help Sheet 225 to help you work out the costs you can claim. If you sell stock you must do your stocktaking at the end of the year and work out how much of your stock was actually sold.

Boxes 3.18 and 3.34

There are special taxation rules for the construction industry. Ask your tax office for advice.

Boxes 3.19 and 3.35: Other direct costs

This will include items that are not classed as 'cost of sales' or running costs or 'business expenses'. *Direct* means the costs are an integral part of providing your goods or services – for instance leasing of milk quotas if you are a farmer – rather than hiring staff which is classed as a running cost. If you are in doubt ask your tax office or make a note in the Additional information box at the end of the Tax Return.

Box 3.36: Gross profit (loss)

Deduct your cost of sales and direct costs (and subcontractor costs if you are in the construction industry) from your turnover to give your gross profit or loss. **Losses must always be written in brackets, not with a minus sign.**

Box 3.37: Other income

This includes income that does not come from sales of goods or services and is not included in your turnover (your sales figure). Do not forget to watch out for income that will be included elsewhere on your Tax Return. For instance bank and building society interest is not trading income. If you include the figure here make a note in box **3.56** so it can be deducted from your profits. Make sure you then include the same figure on page 3 of your main Tax Return under bank and building society interest. Other income can be from rents – if you rent out part of your business premises – and do not include this item on the Land and property pages.

Boxes 3.20 to 3.50: Business expenses

In the total expenses box write the total amount of business expenses **including** ones that you are **not** allowed to claim, such as business entertaining. Then deduct the **disallowable** expenses and put them in the left hand column.

A list of what you are and are not allowed to deduct is given on page SE5 of the Inland Revenue notes on Self-employment. An additional list is given on Help Sheet IR221 (which you should request if you do not already have it).

The only boxes you may find confusing are:

Boxes 3.31 and 3.49: Depreciation and loss/(profit) on sale

These two boxes should both contain the depreciation in value of assets (such as business equipment) and losses incurred when these assets are sold. However, you are not allowed to deduct these as a business expense. As such the figures in both boxes should be the same – and cancel each other out. If you sold assets at a profit deduct this profit from your other losses and depreciation. Only include *fixed assets*. These will be listed on your *balance sheet* (the list of what you own and owe) if you have one. Fixed assets are items which are permanently necessary for your business such as machinery, your business premises or the lease on them. Do not include stock or cash. To calculate depreciation you will need a valuation. If you have a car look in one of the guides to car values on sale in book shops and some newsagents.

Tax tip: If you make a payment that covers an expense for more than one accounting period (for instance 12 months of rent) only deduct the proportion that relates to the accounting period on your Tax Return.

Box 3.51: Total expenses

Add up your total expenses boxes (this should include disallowable expenses).

Box 3.52: Net profit/(loss)

This is your gross profit/(loss) plus other income/profits minus expenses.

TAX ADJUSTMENTS TO NET PROFIT OR LOSS

Box 3.53: Disallowable expenses

These are now added to your net profit as they are not tax deductible and as such have to be added to your taxable profits. Do not forget to include boxes **3.17** to **3.19** at the top of the column.

Box 3.54

If you included the price you paid for goods taken out for personal use (or for friends and family) in your turnover deduct this before writing in the normal selling price of all goods taken out for such use.

Box 3.56: Deductions from net profits

This covers an assortment of extras that are included elsewhere on your Tax Return (so they do not need to be taxed again under self-employment) and taxes you have already paid (you will not want to be taxed twice) .

Deduct from profits (or add to losses) anything that is included in another part of your Tax Return (for instance bank and building society interest), or anything that has already been taxed or is not liable to tax.

If you have income from abroad that has already been taxed and you want to claim tax credit relief you should write in the amount of foreign income you have received in box **3.56** and then include this income on the Foreign pages. Or you can simply claim back foreign pay by putting the amount of income received after tax was deducted. If you include a figure in this box you must explain why in the Additional information box.

Box 3.57

Follow the instructions on the Tax Return to get your net business profit or loss.

Boxes 3.58 to 3.67: Capital allowances and balancing charges

For details of how to work these out see the section earlier in this chapter. During the transitional year 1996 to 1997 the rules covering capital allowances are slightly different.

If you started in business on or after 6 April 1994 you should not be affected by the change from preceding year to current year accounting. So calculate your capital allowances in the usual way. However, if you have more than one business and more than one set of accounts you will be required to do a separate calculation on your second set of self-employment pages.

If you started in business before 6 April 1994 you need to do an additional calculation. However only fill this in on **one** set of self-employment pages (the one you have filled in with your most recent set of accounts). To prevent your capital allowances being reduced in line with your profits (so you do not lose out on the full tax deduction from these allowances) follow these steps:

❑ **Step 1**. Calculate your capital allowances for the two years in the normal way (as described on page 77).

❑ **Step 2**. Take the capital allowance figure you have worked out for the **first** of your basis period years. Then work out the *written down value* of your assets at the end of your 1995/1996 accounting period. Include any new items of capital expenditure and the proceeds of the sale of any capital items.

❑ **Step 3**. Work out the same calculation for the second accounting year in the transitional period. Take the written down value for 1995/1996 and add the cost of assets bought in the 1996/1997 accounting year and deduct the value of any assets sold or scrapped.

❑ **Step 4**. Only now once you have added these figures together do you calculate the 25 per cent capital allowance to include on your Tax Return. Remember some capital allowances can only be claimed at 4 per cent.

This last figure is the amount to write in boxes **3.58**, **3.60**, **3.62** and **3.64**.

You must do a separate calculation (following Steps 1 to 4) for each type of asset. In the other capital allowances box include any items that are not included in the first three boxes.

Balancing charges are not calculated in the same way. Simply add up the balancing charges for the two years covered by the transitional period. This will simply be the 'profit' you made when they were sold – the difference between the price you received on the sale and the written down value. If you make a loss (sell an asset for less than its written down value) write the figure in brackets and do not forget to deduct it from your profits in box **3.76** instead of adding it.

ADJUSTMENTS TO ARRIVE AT TAXABLE PROFIT OR LOSS

Boxes 3.68 and 3.69: Income tax basis period

This will be your **basis period** which may cover more than one accounting period. You need to fill this in so that the Inland Revenue knows that you have adjusted your profits correctly.

BUSINESSES SET UP BEFORE 6 APRIL 1994

Boxes 3.70 and 3.71

You may have more than one accounting period covered by the transitional rules (1995–1996 and 1996–1997). You must add up the total profits of **both** these years and enter them in box **3.70**. So you will have to look at your second set of Self-employment pages (if you have completed them) and add up boxes **3.57** on both of these forms (or boxes **3.13** if you have a turnover of under £15,000).

Then for box **3.71** calculate your transitional average as explained earlier in this chapter. If your basis period is 24 months add up your profits for the two accounting years and multiply them by $^{12}/_{24}$ (or halve them).

If you make a loss enter '0'. You do not have to adjust losses over the transitional period – only profits.

Boxes 3.72 and 3.79

These boxes are for farmers or market gardeners, who can average two years' profits because their income and profits vary from year to year. If you fall into this category and have not already asked for Help Sheet IR224, do so now.

Boxes 3.73 and 3.74

Simply copy the figures from your capital allowances and balancing charges boxes.

Boxes 3.80 and 3.81

Take the adjusted profits figure in box **3.71** then:

❑   add any balancing charges;
❑   deduct any negative balancing charges (losses on the sale of capital assets);
❑   and deduct any capital allowances.

This gives you your net profit for 1996/1997.

If you make a loss simply write '0' in the profits box and write the loss in box **3.81**.

BUSINESSES SET UP ON OR AFTER 6 APRIL 1994

Box 3.75

Remember to add up profits on both self-employment forms if you have filled in more than one set of pages because you have more than one set of accounts.

Boxes 3.76 and 3.77

Simply copy the figures from your capital allowances and balancing charges boxes.

Box 3.78

You will **not** need to fill in this box if your accounting year has not been changed and is 12 months. But if your accounting year has changed or your basis period is not the same as the accounting period you will need to adjust your profits or losses. This has been explained earlier in the chapter. Also read Help Sheet IR222.

Boxes 3.80/3.81

Take the figure in box **3.75** and deduct any capital allowances in box **3.77**, add any balancing charges (deduct these if they are a negative amount or you made a loss on the sale of capital assets) in box **3.76** and then deduct or add any adjustments in boxes **3.78** and **3.79**. Put the final figure in box **3.80**. If you have made a loss write '0' and put the loss in box **3.81**.

LOSSES

Box 3.82

You can offset losses against other income. So you can reduce your tax liability on investments or earnings from employment. Put the amount you want to offset in this box. If your business was set up before 6 April 1994 ask your tax office for advice on how much you can offset.

Box 3.83

You do not have to offset losses against income earned in 1996/1997. **You can use your losses to reduce your tax bill for earlier years.** This is known as carry back. Again, businesses set up before 6 April 1994 should ask their tax office for advice. If you have already made a claim to offset this loss include the figure here and provide the details in the Additional information box.

Box 3.84

You can offset losses against future tax bills. This is known as carrying forward. Write the amount you want to carry forward here.

Boxes 3.85, 3.86 and 3.87

As described above you can use losses to reduce profits (and thus your tax bill) in earlier and future years. This is where you write in any previous losses that you have carried or brought forward. If you want to offset some or all of these against this year's profits write the figure in box **3.86**. Then deduct it from your profits in box **3.80** to give your taxable profit after losses.

Boxes 3.88 and 3.89

Add in any other business income from Enterprise Allowance or Business Start-up Allowance and any other amounts not included elsewhere in the Self-employment pages and include them in box **3.88**. A note in the Additional information box on page 4 of the

Self-employment pages will prevent the tax office asking about this. Then calculate your total taxable profits from this business.

CLASS 4 NATIONAL INSURANCE CONTRIBUTIONS

These payments are collected by the Inland Revenue because they are based on the profits you make from your trade or profession. Note: you can no longer claim half your contributions against tax.

You do not have to pay Class 4 contributions if:

❑ your profits are below the lower profits limit listed in Table 4.5;
❑ you were a man aged over 65 or a woman aged over 60 at 6 April 1996;
❑ you were aged under 16 at 6 April 1996 (provided you have been granted an exception by the Contributions Agency);
❑ or you are not resident in the UK for tax purposes during 1996/1997 (you may be filling in this Tax Return for self-employment earnings in earlier years).

Tax tip: If you are both employed and self-employed you may not have to pay Class 4 National Insurance contributions.

If you already pay the set annual maximum of National Insurance contributions, which is **£2152.86** (which you will if you are an employee **and** earned £455 or more a week in 1996/1997) you should ask the Department of Social Security for a deferral. See the Contributions Agency entry in the telephone directory for the telephone number. If you cannot claim a deferral in advance, Class 4 National Insurance will be deducted from your self-employment earnings and you will then have to claim a repayment. To help you plan ahead, the earnings limits for 1997/1998 are also included in Table 4.5.

The £2152.86 limit applies to all types of National Insurance including Class 4. So if, once Class 4 National Insurance contributions have been deducted from your self-employment profits, you have paid more than £2152.86 in National Insurance contributions you should claim a rebate.

If you do not have to pay Class 4 National Insurance contributions or you have asked for a deferral tick box **3.90** and put a '0' in box **3.92**. Give an explanation as to why you do not need to pay National Insurance in the Additional information box.

If you run more than one business you should also make sure that you do not pay more than the maximum. Ask for Help Sheet IR220.

Box 3.91

You only pay National Insurance on profits and you can offset losses from earlier years if they have not already been used to reduce the profits on which you pay National Insurance. You can also deduct interest earned on savings or bank balances from your profits as you do not pay National Insurance on non-trading income. **So you only have to work out the amount of National Insurance contributions on this reduced profit figure.** *Note*: the profit figure you use in calculating your National Insurance contributions is the one in box **3.89** – after the transitional period averaging calculation.

Box 3.92

Work out your National Insurance using the figures in Table 4.5. **If you do not want to calculate the amount of National Insurance you have to pay, the tax office will do this for you.** Leave box **3.92** blank.

These are the National Insurance rates you must pay on profits and the thresholds at which they become payable. This box does not cover Class 2 contributions that are paid by the self-employed at a flat rate.

Table 4.5 *National Insurance rates*

Self-Employed Class 4 Contributions	1996/1997	1997/1998
Lower profits limit (per year) – no NI contributions payable on profits below this limit	£6860.00	£7010.00
Upper profits limit (per year) – no NI contributions payable on profits above this limit	£23,660.00	£24,180.00
Rate of all contributions payable	6%	6%

These contributions are only paid on profits and gains above the lower threshold and you do not pay any contributions on earnings above the threshold.

So the maximum Class 4 National Insurance contributions paid by the self-employed in 1996/1997 will be:

£23,660 – £6860 = £16,800 (amount between the lower and upper limits) × 6 per cent = **£1008.**

Box 3.93

This relates to the construction industry only and then only to sub-contractors who have had tax deducted at source.

SUMMARY OF BALANCE SHEET

Boxes 3.94 to 3.110

You only need to fill this in if you have a balance sheet. This section is not used to calculate your tax bill.

ADDITIONAL INFORMATION

Explain any figures or accounting decisions here. This may answer questions that your tax office has and prevent them mounting an investigation into your accounts.

5

PARTNERSHIPS

You must fill in the Partnership pages of your Tax Return if you had at any time during the April 1996 to April 1997 tax year a share of profits, losses or income from a business which you carried out in partnership. This also covers income, profits and losses to which you were entitled – so even if you took no money out of the Partnership you must still fill in the pages.

There are two types of Partnership pages to fill in. The short version is for those whose only partnership income was:

❑ a share of trading or professional income;

❑ interest with tax deducted from banks, building societies or deposit takers.

The long or full version covers all possible types of partnership income.

Which of these you fill in will depend not only on what type of income you receive but also on the *partnership statement* you may receive covering your partnership accounts.

This chapter deals with the short version. You will need separate partnership pages for each partnership you are in and for each business the partnership carries on.

WHAT YOU SHOULD NOT INCLUDE

Only include profits while you were in partnership. So if you have changed from being self-employed to being a partner you should include partnership profits on the Partnership pages and self-employed profits on the Self-employment pages.

If you have made a capital gain from the disposal of partnership assets this should be included in the Capital gains pages.

Pension payments are dealt with on page 5 of your main Tax Return.

HOW TAX ON PARTNERSHIPS IS CHANGING

Partners face three changes in the tax system this year:

❑ the change from tax on the partnership to tax on the individual partner;

❑ the change from preceding year to current year accounting; and

❑ Self Assessment.

To know how these changes will affect you, you must first find out if you are an old partnership or a new one. Partnerships are taxed differently if they **started before 6 April 1994**. These are known as *'old partnerships'*. However, if the membership of your partnership changed on or after 6 April 1994 you will be classed as a *'new partnership'* (**unless** you elected for a continuation) along with all partnerships set up on or after this date.

When you join or leave a partnership, legally one partnership comes to an end and another begins even though the business carries on uninterrupted. To avoid this upheaval a partnership can elect for a *continuation*. This means that the business continues to be treated as though it had carried on as usual. Only if the business ceases to trade does the partnership come to an end. The time limit for applying for a continuation is two years from the date of the change. So if you have had a recent change of partners it will be important for you to decide if you want a continuation.

> **T**ax tip: It may be wise to remain as an *old partnership* as you will benefit from the change to current year taxation.

Tax will be paid by the individual partner

In the past partnerships completed and filed a partnership return (Form 1) each year, the Inland Revenue looked at each individual partner's tax return and then worked out the tax rates applicable to each partner's share of the profit. The figures were added together and one tax bill was sent to the partnership for payment.

As from 1996/1997 this changes. It is the last year in which an old partnership will pay tax. And it is the first year in which each partner starts to assess his or her tax liability as an individual. As from 1997/1998 each partner will be charged tax in his or her own right. There will no longer be a tax assessment on the partnership – just on the individual partners.

Old partnerships

Partners in *old partnerships* will **not** need to pay partnership tax themselves until 1997/1998. During the switch from one system to the other the partnership tax will be treated as tax deducted at source. That way you will **not** pay tax twice – once as a partnership and once as an individual. The partnership will pay the tax including the final tax payment for 1996/1997 which is due on 31 January 1998. You should include your share of the tax paid in box **4.74**. You will probably have to wait until the partnership assessment is known before filling in the final figure. The Inland Revenue will need all the individual partners' Tax Returns and the Partnership Tax Return to finalise the tax assessment but will do this quickly so you can fill in your own tax bill. If you want the Inland Revenue to calculate your tax bill, you will need your partnership return by early September so you can fill in your Tax Return and send it back by 30 September.

From 31 January 1998 you will have to make your first tax payment as an individual partner – this will be the first instalment or *payment on account* for the 1997/1998 tax year. This will apply to both *old partnerships* and *new partnerships*. As many partners will not have had to make payments such as these in the past, you are advised to read the introductory section of the Self-employment chapter as in future you will be taxed along the lines of the self-employed.

You will then pay two tax instalments next year – one on 31 January 1988 and the other on 31 July 1998. These instalments will be advance payments on your tax for the 1997/1998 tax year. The payments *on account* will each be half the tax you pay for the 1996/1997 tax year.

Although the partnership will no longer be a taxpaying entity, it will still have to file a partnership return by 31 January 1998 and by the same date every year thereafter. If the partnership fails to send its Tax Return in, a fine of £100 will be imposed on each partner.

New partnerships

New partnerships will not have to provide a partnership tax assessment this year or pay tax as a partnership although the partnership must still send in a Tax Return. The information in the Partnership Tax Return will be used to check that you have correctly filled in your tax due. Your partnership will **not** pay your tax bill. You are responsible for it from now on.

THE CHANGE FROM PRECEDING YEAR TO CURRENT YEAR TAXATION

Partners are broadly taxed in the same way as sole traders and will calculate their tax liability during 1996/1997 in the same way as the self-employed. **Old partnerships** will have to change from *preceding year* taxation, under which they were taxed on profits made in the accounting year ending in the previous tax year. In future they will be taxed on a *current year* basis – taxed on the accounting year ending in the tax year just ended.

These terms and what they mean are fully explained in the Self-employment chapter. But to sum up, if you have an accounting year end of 31 December you would normally include profits to 31 December 1995 on your 1996/1997 Tax Return (the one sent out in April 1997). This year you switch to current year accounting and you must also include your profits to 31 December 1996. So there will be two sets of accounts and twice the amount of profits, but not twice the amount of tax. The transitional rules mean that profits for the two accounting years are added together on your 1996/1997 Tax Return and usually halved. **This means that the tax due for each of these years is also halved**. These changes will only affect **old partnerships.**

If you are a *new partner* in an old partnership you will find that you will **not** benefit from the transitional rules which could halve your tax. You will be taxed on a share of partnership profits for the first tax year in which you are a partner or the most recent accounting period. If you have *left an old partnership* you will not be taxed on the last year's profits even though they are credited to your capital account.

FILLING IN YOUR PARTNERSHIP TAX PAGES

If you need the full version of the Partnership pages to declare income from foreign savings, offshore funds, land and property, furnished holiday lettings and other income not included in the short version, ask your tax office to send you a copy of these pages. The full version has 75 boxes (compared to 29 on the short version) but it is unlikely that all of them will apply to you.

PAPERWORK REQUIRED

You will need your Partnership returns and accounts; the Inland Revenue notes on Partnerships; and any relevant Help Sheets listed at the beginning of the Inland Revenue notes. Filling in the forms is much easier than for the self-employed as you can rely on your Partnership accounts for the information.

Boxes 4.1–4.4

Box 4.1 refers to your partnership tax reference number which should be at the top of your previous partnership Tax Return. The rest of the information required is straightforward. Do not forget you should fill in these boxes for every set of partnership pages you have. So if your partnership has more than one business or you are in more than one partnership you will need two forms.

You should get all the information you need from the partner nominated to be responsible for the Partnership Tax Return.

Tax payment dates: These will change from 1 January and 1 July 1997 to 31 January and 31 July 1998 for old partnerships.

Boxes 4.5 and 4.6

These only apply to new partnerships. To know what date to fill in you must find out your *basis period*. To do this you must know your *accounting date* – the date your accounts are drawn up at the end of your Partnership's 12-month accounting year. The Income Tax *basis period* will usually be your last accounting period.

If your partnership **started between 6 April 1994 and 5 April 1995** your basis period is the 12 months to your accounting date.

If your partnership started between **6 April 1995 and 5 April 1996** and your accounts are drawn up less than 12 months after the date you started **do not** use the accounting date. Instead, put down your first 12 months of trading in partnership.

If the accounting date in the April 1996 to April 1997 tax year is 12 months or more after the date on which you started in business, put down the 12 months to your accounting date.

If you do not have an accounting date in 1996/1997 your basis period is the same 12 months as the tax year.

If you have not been in partnership for 12 months, put down the date you started and end your basis period on 5 April 1997 (the end of the tax year).

If you have changed accounting dates you may have a longer accounting or basis period. And if you are no longer a partner special rules apply. The basis period rules for businesses started on or after 6 April 1994 in Chapter 4 on Self-employment also apply to partnerships. These will tell you if you have a different basis period to your last accounting period. See Help Sheet IR222 for more information.

Boxes 4.7 and 4.8

If you are in an **old partnership** simply enter the profit allocated to you in your 1996/1997 partnership assessment (given to you by your partnership accountant or the partner responsible for your tax) in box **4.7.** You do not have to do any calculations. Enter '0' if you made a loss.

If you are a member of a new partnership you may have to adjust your profits.

If you are in a **new partnership** and your *basis period* is the same as the partnership's accounting year simply copy the profit figure from your Partnership Tax Return and write this in box **4.7.** You can leave box **4.8** blank.

However, if your *basis period* is different to the partnerships' accounting period you will have to do a calculation.

If more than one partnership accounting period ends in the April 1996 to April 1997 tax year combine the two figures for your share of the partnership's profits or losses. Write this figure in box **4.7**. If no accounting period ends in 1996–1997 write '0'.

Then in box **4.8** adjust the profit or loss in **4.7** so that only profits made in the *basis period* are included.

If your *basis period profits* are less than your partnership's profits in box **4.7** you will have to make a deduction in box **4.8**. This will be the difference between the two figures and the amount should be written in brackets.

If your *basis period profits* as calculated above are greater than the partnership profits in box **4.7** you must calculate the difference and write it in box **4.8**.

You should also include any overlap relief in box **4.8**. Overlap profits can occur in the first few years of a partnership and when accounting dates are changed. The term means that profits were taxed twice. If you have any overlap relief from 1995/1996 or earlier years include it here to reduce the amount of taxable profits for 1996/1997. See Chapter 4 on Self-employment for more details.

Box 4.9

If you are a **new partnership** which carries on a farming business you may be able to claim to average your share of two years' profits. Ask for Help Sheet IR224.

You can also use this box to claim tax back if it has been deducted from foreign earnings. If you do not do this here, you can include it on the Foreign pages (but not on both pages).

Boxes 4.10 and 4.11

Adjust the profit or loss figure in **4.7** by adding or subtracting boxes **4.8** and **4.9**. If you have made a profit enter it in **4.11**. If you have made a loss put it in box **4.12** and write '0' in box **4.11**.

Boxes 4.12 to 4.16

This enables you to offset losses made in 1996 to 1997 against other income (for instance tax on your employment earnings or your private income from land and property). You can also offset losses the partnership made in previous years against this year's tax bill or carry losses forward to future years.

If you are using losses to reduce your profits this year, deduct them from your net profit figure in box **4.10** to give your taxable profit after losses.

Box 4.18

Any other income that needs to be included to calculate your profits has to be entered here. See your Partnership Tax Return.

Box 4.19

The total taxable profits: you will have to pay tax on these yourself if you are in a new partnership as the tax bill will no longer be settled by the partnership.

Box 4.20: National Insurance

See the notes in Chapter 4 on Self-employment. The same rules apply. But instead of paying National Insurance on the total business or partnership profits, those in partnership only pay National Insurance on their share of the profits.

Other boxes

The remaining boxes can be copied from your Partnership Tax Return. You do not have to worry about applying the basis period to box **4.69**. Taxed income from savings is calculated over the year to 5 April 1997 and no adjustment needs to be made.

6

LAND AND PROPERTY

These pages have to be filled in by anyone who received income from land and property in the tax year 6 April 1996 to 5 April 1997 – even if your rent is tax free under the Rent-a-Room rules.

Income from renting out a holiday home **overseas** should be entered on the Foreign pages.

If you received income from land and property that was owned by a partnership, that income should be included in the Partnership pages.

Land and property also includes rents from *immobile caravans* and permanent *houseboats*.

CHANGES AS A RESULT OF SELF ASSESSMENT

Tax on property income in the 1995 to 1996 tax year was payable on 1 January 1996. This was before the end of the tax year so you did not always know your final figure. You may have had to pay a second bill later in the year.

Under Self Assessment this will change. You will now have three payment dates if you owe more than £500 in tax. There will be two interim payments known as payments *on account* on 31 January (during the tax year) and 31 July (just after the end of the tax year) and a final settling payment (to adjust for any over- or underpaid tax) on 31 January the year after. In other cases there will be just one payment date on 31 January, but this will be the January after the tax year ends, not the January during the tax year. So tax on rental income earned in the 1996/1997 tax year will not be due until January 1998.

PAPERWORK REQUIRED

It is essential for you to keep accurate and detailed records if you are to make the most of the expenses you can deduct from your income to reduce your tax bill. Make sure you have all your accounts to hand, records of rent received and any bills relating to the rented property or land. These should include:

- ❑ rent, rates, insurance, ground rents, service charges, etc;
- ❑ any bills for repairs and maintenance;
- ❑ your mortgage interest statements or other loan details;
- ❑ any bills you have for legal, accountancy, surveying and other costs;
- ❑ details of any wages you have paid out.

> **Warning:** Before starting to fill in these pages make sure your accounts cover the same period as the tax year. If they do not, you will have to recalculate them so you only include income and expenses received and incurred during the tax year.

THE RENT-A-ROOM SCHEME

This is the scheme that allows you to rent out a room in your home and receive up to £3250 a year – or £62.50 a week – tax free from 6 April 1996 to 5 April 1997.

This only applies if the room is furnished, it is in your only or main home, and you do not run this as a business (such as a guest house).

You can only rent out **one** room and get the full £3250 allowance. You cannot try to claim two lots of allowance by getting someone else in your home to rent out a room. If two rooms are let in the same property, one by you and one by someone you jointly-own the property with, the allowance is halved to £1625.

If you receive £3250 or less from renting out a room, tick the *yes* box on the top of the land and property page. There is no point in taking up the option of working out your profit as all of this rental income is tax free.

If you earn **more** than £3250 in rent you can either claim the Rent-a-Room allowance and pay tax on the amount of rent over this limit **or** be taxed on your rental profits. Your profits will be the amount you receive in rent minus the expenses. In most cases you will be better off claiming the allowance. Only work out the rental profits if your expenses are more than £3250. See the other land and property income section of this chapter for a list of the type of expenses you can deduct. From the 1997/1998 tax year this allowance rises to £4250.

Tax tip: If your home is jointly owned, look at the tax advantages of splitting your Rent-a-Room Allowance if your rent exceeds the £3250 limit. If your spouse, or whoever else jointly owns your home, pays tax at a lower rate you will be better off splitting the rent so half of it is taxed at a lower rate.

FURNISHED HOLIDAY LETTINGS

To qualify as furnished holiday lettings, the property must be:

- ❏ furnished;
- ❏ available for holiday letting to the public at a commercial rent for 140 days or more during the year;
- ❏ actually let commercially as holiday accommodation for 70 days or more during the year;
- ❏ not occupied continuously for more than 31 days by the same person in any seven month period.

See page L2 of your tax notes for further details.

If you rent out an immovable caravan this is also classed as a furnished holiday letting provided it meets the above criteria.

If you own and let holiday property with one or more other people only include your share of rent and your share of expenses.

> **T**ax tip: If your holiday letting nearly fits these criteria, make sure it does next year. There are tax advantages. For a start, if you make any losses you can use this to reduce your tax bill on earnings from employment or profits from self-employment. You cannot do this with other rental income, you can only use losses to offset other property profits. Furnished holiday lettings have other tax advantages. You can claim capital allowances (a proportion of the amount you spend) on furniture, fixtures and fittings. With other types of rental income you can only claim for *wear and tear* of these items or the cost of replacing them. But you cannot claim capital allowances **and** replacement costs – only one or the other.

You do not have to itemise expenses or fill in boxes **5.2** to **5.7** if your rental income is less than £15,000 a year. Just fill in the total amount claimed. A full list of what can be deducted is included in the 'Other property income' section of this chapter.

Box 5.10: private use

If you buy anything for your rented property that is also partly for private use you should put the **total** amount spent in the expenses boxes and then deduct the value of the proportion that was for private use here.

Boxes 5.16–5.18: Losses

As discussed above furnished holiday lettings are the only type of rental income you can use to offset losses against other income **and** capital gains. You can also use losses in this year **to reduce your tax bill in an earlier year.**

Also fill in box **5.19** overleaf, but do **not** fill in boxes **5.24** to **5.30** if you do not have any other income from rental property.

OTHER PROPERTY INCOME

This covers all property income other than furnished holiday lettings and the Rent-A-Room scheme (unless you want to opt out of this and be taxed on rental profits in the usual way). This broad category includes everything from leasing out acres of land to renting your property out to a film crew.

Do **not** include income from Enterprise Zone trusts as these go on page 3 of your main Tax Return.

Remember the rent is classed as being received when you earned it, **not** when you actually get paid. If you have a bad debt that you cannot recover reasonably you can deduct this. Put this in box **5.29** (or box **5.70** if a furnished holiday let). And if you are paid in advance for rent and some of this relates to the period after 5 April 1997, this does not have to be included. You cannot evade tax by taking payment in kind – if, for instance, you are given the free use of a car or other goods or services.

If your income is from the granting of a lease see page L5 of the Inland Revenue notes for special rules.

Expenses

Do not itemise these if your total property income is less than £15,000 annually. But you will still need to know what are allowable expenses.

You cannot deduct the cost of buying the land or property or the cost of machinery, furnishings or furniture or any losses you make when you sell the land or property. But you can deduct any expenses 'wholly and exclusively' incurred in renting your land and property.

- ❑ Any rent you pay to someone else for the use of the land or property.
- ❑ Council Tax, business rates, ground rents.
- ❑ Heat and light (gas and electricity).
- ❑ Insurance against loss of rent.
- ❑ Insuring the property.
- ❑ Maintenance and repairs from painting to roof repairs (but not a new roof) and damp treatments, but not any improvements to the property.
- ❑ **Interest on a loan to buy your property** and any costs incurred in arranging the loan.
- ❑ Legal and professional costs of letting a property for a **year or less**.

- ❑ Accountancy fees for drawing up your accounts.
- ❑ The costs of collecting rent.
- ❑ The costs of evicting a tenant.
- ❑ The costs of travelling/motoring to visit your property – but not if you combine this with a holiday or private trip.
- ❑ Management expenses as a landlord – telephone calls, stationery, travelling for business purposes.
- ❑ The costs of providing additional services such as cleaning and gardening.
- ❑ Advertising, estate agent and accommodation agency fees.
- ❑ **Either** *wear and tear:* you cannot claim the purchase costs of equipment or furniture in a let residential property (unless it is a furnished holiday let) as an allowable expense. However, you can claim 10 per cent for wear and tear of fixtures, fittings, cookers, even lampshades, beds and sheets. The figures are worked out using the rent you receive less service charges and water rates. You deduct 10 per cent of this figure to give your wear and tear allowance. So over ten years you should be able to recoup most of the initial costs.
- ❑ **Or** *replacement and renewal:* this allows you to claim the full cost of replacing furniture, furnishings and household equipment – but only when you need to replace them.

You have to choose between renewal expenses and wear and tear. You cannot have both and, once you have chosen a basis, you must stick to it. You cannot claim renewal expenses or wear and tear on items on which you have claimed a capital allowance.

You cannot claim for:

- ❑ The costs of your own time.
- ❑ The costs of buying the property (only loan interest).
- ❑ The costs of improving the property (this is deducted as a cost when you sell to reduce your Capital Gains Tax liability).

Make sure you keep all receipts so you can tax deduct every expense incurred *wholly and exclusively* for the purpose of your rental business. This will include light bulbs, bed linen and cleaning fluids.

Tax tip: MIRAS: if it is your only or main home that you are renting out (say while you are working overseas) you may still be able to claim MIRAS – mortgage interest tax relief at source – which gives you 15 per cent tax relief on interest payments made on the first £30,000 of your home loan. Alternatively you can claim all the interest as an allowable expense and opt out of MIRAS. This will give you a bigger saving unless your rents are very low.

Boxes 5.11, 5.12, 5.33 and 5.36

Capital allowances enable you to tax deduct some of the purchase price of items you use in letting your property. **These cannot include furniture or household equipment unless the property is classed as a furnished holiday let.** However, if the property is not a furnished home (it is a commercial property) you **can** claim capital allowances on furniture, fixtures and fittings. All landlords can deduct the cost of any machinery or equipment used in maintaining the property such as ladders, tools and even garden equipment such as lawnmowers. You can also claim for the cost of constructing agricultural buildings, industrial and commercial buildings in Enterprise Zones and certain types of hotel.

This capital allowance will be 25 per cent of the initial purchase price in the first year of ownership.

If this is £10,000 you can deduct 25 per cent as a capital allowance = **£2500.**

In the second year you can deduct 25 per cent of the remaining value or *written down value*:

£10,000 – £2500 (already claimed) = £7500 (the written down value).
So you can deduct 25 per cent of £7500 = **£1875.**

This capital allowance calculation continues until the item is no longer of use. You then add the figure you have left as the written down value as a *balancing charge*. Or if you sell the item for more than the written down value, include the amount you receive from the sale in box **5.11.** You will be taxed on this 'profit'.

To save calculating each item separately you can *pool* the written down values and just deduct 25 per cent in one go. When you buy extra items simply add them to the pool.

If you buy an item on hire purchase, you can claim capital allowances on the original cost of the item. The interest and other charges are classed as expenses and should be deducted in boxes **5.4** and **5.26**.

If you opt for the renewal and replacement option you **cannot** claim for the initial purchase costs. So you cannot claim a capital allowance **and** for the cost of replacement on the same item.

Tax tip: If an item that was previously for private use is now used in your business you can claim a capital allowance on its market value when you start using it for business.

If you only use items partly for business or want to know any more about capital allowances ask for Help Sheet IR250. If you want to claim agricultural buildings allowance ask for Help Sheet IR224.

TAX ADJUSTMENTS

As from 6 April 1995 all property you let is treated as one type of business and all income and expenses are aggregated (added together) so you can offset one type of property loss against another (other than losses on overseas properties). Only losses from furnished holiday lets can be offset against other types of income (for instance income from employment or self-employment).

However, all rental losses can be *carried forward*. This means you can use your losses this year to reduce your profits from rental income in future years.

Agricultural estates or land managed as one estate are treated differently. Ask for Help Sheet IR 251.

Warning: When you sell a property that has been let out you may have to pay Capital Gains Tax on the profit. This may also be charged if you let part of your main home. See Chapter 9 on Capital Gains.

7

FOREIGN INCOME

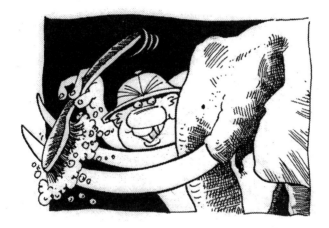

Do not confuse this with Non-residence. Foreign income covers income from overseas whereas Non-residence is for those who live overseas.

This chapter covers savings that are in overseas or offshore accounts, dividends from overseas shares, offshore investment funds, overseas pensions and social security benefits and any income you receive from land and property, including overseas holiday homes that you let out.

The **Self Assessment** system allows you to calculate your own tax and also means that you will pay tax on different dates in future. Instead of paying on 1 January for the year being assessed (before you have filled in your Tax Return) you will make up to three payments. From next year these will be:

❏ 31 January 1998 for any outstanding tax owed for the 1996/1997 tax year;

❏ 31 January 1998 for the first instalment of tax for the 1997/1998 year; and

❏ 31 July 1998 for the second instalment of tax for the 1997/1998 year (these two instalments are known as payments 'on account').

If you have any outstanding tax for the 1997/1998 tax year this will be payable on 31 January 1999.

However, if you receive a small proportion of your income from overseas (if over 89 per cent of your income is from PAYE or you owe less than £500 in tax) you will only have **one payment date**, 31 January 1998.

PAPERWORK REQUIRED

You will need any dividend vouchers, bank statements, pensions advice notes, foreign tax assessments and receipts for foreign tax paid. If you invest in an overseas unit trust or investment fund you will need your fund voucher. If you have a property overseas you will also need to have all your receipts for expenses – from the cost of your mortgage to maintenance and care-taking bills. The guidance notes from the Inland Revenue (which you should ask for if you have not received them) are 22 pages long but only because each country has a different tax arrangement (or Treaty) with the UK and these are listed in full.

You will need a calculator to help you convert all income into sterling.

These pages will enable you to reclaim any foreign Income Tax deducted on your overseas income. You can also reclaim Capital Gains Tax paid in a foreign country. You can use this to reduce (offset) some of your UK bill. You can calculate the tax credit yourself by following Part B on the notes provided by the Inland Revenue.

This section does not deal with profits made on the sale of overseas homes or offshore and overseas shares and investments. You must include these on the Capital Gains pages.

Warning: You will be taxed on your foreign income as you earn it, not on the date you bring the money into the UK or are paid it. However, if exchange controls mean you cannot bring the income into the UK it should not be taxable.

All amounts must be listed in sterling and you must use the exchange rate on the day you earned the foreign income (not received it or brought it into the UK). Working out which exchange rate to use can be difficult. Ask your tax office for help.

If you are resident in the UK but not domiciled here for tax purposes or are a citizen of the Commonwealth or the Republic of Ireland, special rules apply. These are the remittance basis rules and cover income you receive in the UK. Ask for the Non-residence pages by ringing the Orderline on 0645 000 404 and read the notes carefully.

If your savings and investments are in *joint names* enter only your share of the income.

Warning: You can only reclaim foreign tax at the official rates agreed. There is a full list in your Inland Revenue guidance notes.

HOW TO CLAIM BACK FOREIGN TAX

If tax has been deducted from your foreign income by an overseas tax authority you can claim back the tax in one of two ways:

❑ by deducting this tax from the amount of income and gains which will be taxed in the UK (put this final figure in box E on the Tax Return); or
❑ by claiming tax credit relief.

This second option is normally the best. However, if the foreign tax is higher than the UK tax, you can only claim *tax credit relief* up to the amount of UK tax you will pay. This tax credit will reduce your tax bill but only on the same type of income – it cannot be used to reduce tax on other types of income.

These rules ensure that you are not taxed twice. However, if you are not liable for UK Income Tax you cannot claim the foreign tax back by using the tax credit system.

If your foreign income is paid to you through a UK agent (eg a bank) tax will already be deducted. The agent should allow for any double taxation agreement.

THE CHANGE TO CURRENT YEAR ACCOUNTING

Self Assessment means that all income will be taxed on a *current year* basis in future, which means you will be taxed on income earned in a year at the end of that year. In the past income (such as interest and dividends) from foreign investments, rents from property, and overseas pensions which you started to receive before **6 April 1994** was taxed on a *preceding year basis*. This meant that income earned in the 6 April 1995 to 5 April 1996 tax year did not have to be included on your Tax Return until 1997. To bring this into line with the current year basis during this transitional year you will have to declare income for the 1995/1996 tax year **and** the 1996/1997 tax year on the April 1997 Tax Return.

This means you will have to include two years of income on your Tax Return. But so that you do not have to pay double the tax you then halve the amount of taxable income in each year using an averaging calculation. **This means you only pay half the tax due on your 1995/1996 and 1996/1997 income.**

Income that is not affected by this change

Only investments which started to earn you income (interest or dividends) before 6 April 1994 are affected. However, some investments made between 6 April 1993 and 5 April 1994 may already be taxed on a current year basis. You will know if this is the case as you will have already paid tax on your 1995 to 1996 income and included these on the Tax Return you received in April 1996.

You may have some income that comes from **pre 6 April 1994 investments** and some that comes from investments made since then. You will have to treat these differently.

If you sold your investment in the year to 5 April 1997, you are not affected by the change to the current year taxation. Instead you will be taxed on the full amount you earned in the year **from** 6 April 1996 to the date it was sold. This applies even if you made the investment before 6 April 1994.

If you receive dividends through a UK collecting agent – in other words with UK tax already paid – you do not have to calculate an averaging figure even if the investment was made before 6 April 1994. Simply write in the gross dividend received in the year to 5 April 1997 and any UK tax and foreign tax paid.

How to calculate your income in the transitional period

Only include income affected by the change to current year taxation. The same *averaging* calculation applies to interest, dividends, **foreign pensions** and **property income**, provided you started to receive it before 6 April 1994 .

❑ Divide the income you received in the 6 April 1995 to 5 April 1996 tax year **and** the 6 April 1996 to 5 April 1997 tax year by 50 per cent (halve it). This is the income to put in column B.

❑ Add up the withholding tax for the two years and divide by 50 per cent (halve it). This is the figure to put in column D.

❑ If you want to claim tax credit relief tick box E and do **not** fill in a figure. If you do not want to claim tax credit relief deduct the figure in column D from the one in column B and write this in box E.

FOREIGN SAVINGS

These include savings, interest and dividends but **not** offshore unit and investment trusts or other offshore funds.

Foreign Income Dividends (FIDS) from UK companies should be included on page 3 of your main Tax Return.

Each block of shares and each savings account is a separate source of income and should be listed separately. Shares bought at different times are also separate entries.

Ignore the unremittable box **unless** you are not domiciled in the UK for tax purposes but live in the UK **or** if you are a citizen of the Commonwealth or Republic of Ireland **and** are resident in the UK.

If you receive dividends from Finland, France, Italy or the Republic of Ireland you may be able to get the other country's tax credit in addition to any dividend. Add this tax credit to the dividend to get the figure to put in box B.

Tax tip: If you hold savings accounts in joint names you can elect to have a larger share apportioned to the partner who pays tax at the lowest rate.

Tax tip: You can get foreign tax reduced or claim another country's tax credit (for instance on dividends) by writing to the Financial Intermediaries and Claims Office (International), Fitzroy House, PO Box 46, Nottingham BG2 1BD or telephoning them on 0115 974 2000.

OVERSEAS PENSIONS AND BENEFITS

If you started to receive your pension (including those from a foreign state) before 6 April 1994 calculate your tax using the *averaging* calculation shown earlier in this chapter.

Some pensions and social security benefits are exempt from UK tax. Read page F7 of your Inland Revenue notes. Also note that only 90 per cent of the pension income from an overseas employer scheme or pension fund is taxed.

Remember if you are **not** claiming a foreign tax credit, deduct any foreign tax from your total pension or benefit (the figure in box B) and write this figure in column E.

LAND AND PROPERTY

You must fill in the relevant section of page F2 **and** page F4. On page F2 leave column C blank. **You only have to declare income brought into the UK.** Therefore you can only claim back any foreign tax in column D on the income brought into the UK (not the total amount of tax paid to the foreign tax authority).

The rules covering pre 6 April 1994 income apply to property income and you must work through the *averaging* calculation earlier in this chapter. You will have to do this if you started to receive rents from your overseas home before 6 April 1994. You must *add together* your income from the 1995 to 1996 tax year **and** the 1996 to 1997 year and then *halve* this. Both years' income must be included on your Tax Return. You must do the same calculation for your expenses – add the two years' expenses together and then halve the figure. A working sheet is included on page F12 of the Inland Revenue notes to help you with your calculations.

However, if you no longer let out your property you will be taxed on a current year basis which means you only need to include income from 6 April 1996 to the date you sold your property or stopped renting it out.

Only rent received or due in the tax year must be included on your Tax Return.

If you have two properties and one was bought on or after 6 April 1994 the newer property will be taxed on a *current year* basis and the other using the averaging rules (the average of two years' profits).

Read Chapter 6 on Land and Property for details of what you can deduct as expenses. Do **not** itemise expenses if your total income in the year before expenses is **less than £15,000**. You will find it very difficult to claim the cost of air fares unless you can prove that the travel was wholly and exclusively for the purposes of the overseas letting business.

> **Tax tip:** You can deduct from your rental income interest you pay on a loan to buy the property abroad (something that was not available before 6 April 1995). But you can only claim a proportion of this if the property was only let for part of the year.

You will need to fill in a separate copy of page F4 for each property.

Do not fill in boxes 6.28 and 6.29 if your property income has been averaged using the transitional period calculation.

If you or your family use your overseas home for part of the year and rent it out for the remainder you must apportion your costs accordingly. The same applies if you only rent out part of the property. So if it is let for six months you can only claim half the costs.

OFFSHORE FUNDS

If you have invested in a unit trust where income is automatically reinvested (roll-over funds) you still have to declare this income. The unit trust company should give you a tax voucher showing if foreign tax was deducted.

Some distributor funds have equalisation arrangements, which means that part of the gain (profit on sale) is subject to Income Tax. Check your redemption voucher. Any amount that is not a gain should be included in box **6.5**. Profits made when you sell investments are usually taxed under Capital Gains Tax.

FOREIGN LIFE INSURANCE POLICIES

Income and gains in most offshore insurance policies do not usually have foreign tax deducted but if it is deducted you **cannot** claim it as a tax credit relief and you cannot use it to reduce your gains in box **6.8**. Life insurance policies are treated as though basic rate tax is deducted. You only have to pay extra tax if you are a higher rate taxpayer.

FOREIGN TAX CREDITS

Page F3 is for you to total up the tax credits you are claiming for foreign tax deducted on income in other sections of your Tax Return including:

❑ employment;
❑ self-employment;
❑ partnerships; or
❑ capital gains.

You can only claim tax credit relief if you have included the tax in the figures you have entered elsewhere. If you have deducted foreign tax before writing in your income, you cannot claim a tax credit as well.

8

TRUSTS

Trusts are a specialist area of tax. However, you do not have to know about trust law as the trust deed will have been drafted by a solicitor. You only have to know how much income you received from a trust. In this case you are the *beneficiary*.

You will also have to fill in this form if you are a *settlor*. This means you have set up a trust fund.

This chapter does not deal with unit or investment trusts. They should be included on your main Tax Return on page 3.

 PAPERWORK REQUIRED

All documentation given to you by the trustee of your trust. If you have received money from the estate of a deceased person you should have a statement of the amounts paid. The estate representative should give you these. Copy this information on to the Trust page. If you are entitled to income from a trust by right (it is not a discretionary trust) you can ask your trustees for a Certificate of Income and Tax Deduction (Form R185E) which will detail the figures you need.

Note: Some trusts are taxable at 34 per cent. These are discretionary trusts (where payments are at the discretion of the trustees and you have no automatic right to these payments) and accumulation trusts (usually set up to avoid or reduce inheritance tax and to pass wealth on to future generations aged under 25 when the trust is set up). The trustees will prepare and submit a Trust and Estate Tax Return, which is designed for both UK resident trusts and the estates of deceased persons. If you receive an income payment from a discretionary or accumulation trust this will carry a tax credit of 34 per cent in 1996/1997.

This shows that 34 per cent tax has been deducted. Any repayment of the tax due will then be given to you once you have filled in your Tax Return. And any additional tax you owe will be added to your total tax liability.

Before filling in the page you will need to know if the income you received is taxable and if it should be included on this page or another part of your Tax Return.

INCOME FROM TRUSTS AND SETTLEMENTS

The term *absolute right to income* means that you get that income automatically, not at the discretion of trustees. These include life interest trusts and interest in possession trusts. Because you have an automatic right to the income, for tax purposes the trust is disregarded. As such you must **not** include certain income on the Trusts page.

Include in section 10 of your main Tax Return:

❑   share dividends from UK companies;
❑   dividends from UK authorised unit trusts;
❑   dividends from investment trusts (open-ended investment companies).

Include all foreign interest and dividends on the foreign pages.

The representative administering the trust should tell you what to include on your Tax Return. Enter in box **7.3** the total income (without tax deducted), put the tax deducted (at 24 per cent or the 34 per cent trust rate) in box **7.2** and the amount you actually received in box **7.1**.

If tax has been deducted at the lower 20 per cent rate (or you have a tax credit at that rate) fill in boxes **7.4** to **7.6**. Tax is deducted at the lower rate on share dividends and building society saving interest.

If there is *no absolute right to income* – for instance from a discretionary trust – you should have received all the information you need from the trustee, who should tell you what types of income have been received on your behalf.

Settlors – those who set up trusts – may also have to declare their income in boxes **7.1** to **7.6**. This will be if you retain an interest in the trust, which means the money could be paid to you in 'any circumstances whatsoever' (however remote the possibility). For instance, the beneficiary dying and the capital being returned to you or the trusts deeds being written in such a way that you or your spouse could become beneficiaries.

You will also have to declare the income if you make a settlement in favour of children under 16 as any income that is paid to them is classed as being for your benefit. However, this will exclude gross (without tax deducted) income of £100 or less a year.

Tax tip: To get round the rules on trusts for the benefit of your children you can get the grandparents to set up the trust.

Because these rules are so wide-ranging, if you are a settlor you should ask for Help Sheet IR270 by ringing the Orderline on 0645 000 404.

INCOME FROM THE ESTATES OF DECEASED PERSONS

This does not include income earned on inheritances and legacies before they are paid to you. Remember, you do not pay tax on inheritances when you receive them. But while the estate is being managed and before you are paid any inheritance the estate may earn interest or rental income from a property. This income is taxed in the relevant section of your Tax Return – for instance savings will be included on page 3 and property income in Land and Property.

Put your other income in the relevant boxes:

❑ Basic rate means 24 per cent tax has been deducted.
❑ Lower rate means 20 per cent has been deducted – for instance from savings interest or share dividends.
❑ Non-repayable means that tax has been deducted and you cannot reclaim this tax.

9

CAPITAL GAINS

You pay Capital Gains Tax if you *sell or dispose of an asset* – a possession, investment or business; and you *receive capital* – a sum of cash; and have *made a gain* – or a profit. You pay the tax on the profit you make, **not** on the amount you receive when you sell the asset.

You are required to fill in the Capital Gains Tax pages if you have made profits (gains) on the sale of assets (investments, second homes, shares, antiques, inheritances) and:

❑ these total more than £12,600 (not each); or
❑ you have made profits of more than £6300 (in total); or
❑ you have sold your main home and you have used this for running a business or have rented it out;
❑ although the tax form does not stipulate this, you should also fill in the Capital Gains Tax pages if you made **losses from the sale of assets**. You can then use these to reduce your tax bill – in this year, past or future years.

Even if you fall into one of these categories you may not have to pay Capital Gains Tax.

 PAPERWORK REQUIRED

It is essential for you to keep accurate and detailed records in order to make sure that you are filling in the right figures. You will have a major problem if you have not kept receipts or statements showing when you bought each item, how much you paid, any costs involved in the purchase, any expenditure to improve the item and how much you sold it for.

You will also need a calculator as you have to do all the calculations yourself: you will probably need to do these on a separate piece of paper.

Tax payment dates: Instead of 1 December payments must be made by the 31 January after the end of the tax year. So that will be 31 January 1998.

ASSETS LIABLE TO CAPITAL GAINS TAX

These include the following:

❑ land (apart from the grounds of your home if they are smaller than one and a quarter acres);
❑ shares;
❑ second homes;
❑ antiques and works of art (unless they are chattels – see below);
❑ unit and investments trusts;
❑ jewellery and silver (unless they are chattels);
❑ the proceeds of a building society takeover or conversion to a bank – you may have to pay Capital Gains Tax on the cash or shares you receive (ask your building society for advice);
❑ gains made in a trust if you are the person who set up the trust (the settlor) and you retain an interest in the trust (can benefit from it);
❑ most things you hold for personal or investment purposes – basically any asset that is not exempt.

ASSETS EXEMPT FROM
CAPITAL GAINS TAX

These include the following:

❑ private cars (unless you sell them for a business or regularly sell them at a profit);

- ❑ your main home (principal private residence) provided you have not let it out or used it for business;
- ❑ personal possessions or chattels (which are each worth £6000)
- ❑ Personal Equity Plans (PEPs);
- ❑ bonuses from TESSA accounts;
- ❑ gilts – UK Government stocks and some corporate bonds bought after 13 March 1984;
- ❑ shares issued under the enterprise investment scheme;
- ❑ British money including post-1837 gold sovereigns;
- ❑ foreign currency for personal use;
- ❑ betting and lottery winnings;
- ❑ life insurance policies (with some exceptions – mainly purchasing from a third party or another person, not the life insurance company);
- ❑ National Savings Investments;
- ❑ venture capital trusts;
- ❑ qualifying corporate bonds (but not on a company share reorganisation or takeover);
- ❑ personal injury compensation;
- ❑ damages including those for defamation or personal injury;
- ❑ decorations for valour that belong to your family (ie your grandfather's George Cross);
- ❑ gifts to charities and certain national institutions;
- ❑ if you are running a business, trading stock that you sell is also exempt;
- ❑ you do not have to pay capital gains tax on money you get as a gift or on money (or an asset) which is taxable as part of your income – or which would be subject to Income Tax;
- ❑ inheritances – however, when you sell an inheritance you may still be liable to Capital Gains Tax on any profits.

Tax tip: To avoid the risk of having to pay Capital Gains Tax on the sale of shares – including shares from a SAYE company share scheme – invest using a Personal Equity Plan (PEP). You can invest up to £3000 each year in a single share PEP and can transfer shares worth up to this amount from profit-sharing schemes, approved savings-related share options schemes (SAYE schemes) and new share issues. You can also invest up to £6000 in a general PEP which, in turn, invests in shares, unit trusts and investment trusts.

Tax tip: Whenever possible you should try to use up your capital gains tax allowance. You can do this by selling assets in part, so you do not make a massive profit in one year or by using a tax avoidance system known as *bed and breakfasting* which enables you to sell shares, unit or investment trusts at the end of the tax year to use up your Capital Gains Tax allowance and then buy the same assets back the next day. Your stockbroker, unit trust or investment trust company will tell you how to do this cheaply. You can also use this to make a deliberate loss. This loss can then reduce any gains you make in that year.

HOW DO I KNOW IF I HAVE MADE A GAIN?

You make a gain if the value of something you sold has risen in value since you bought it (or since 31 March 1982 if you purchased prior to this date). You do not pay tax on the first £6300 of gains (this is the profit on the sale of **all** assets) and you only pay tax on gains above this limit. You will pay Capital Gains Tax at your top rate of tax.

You may make a capital gain even if you do not sell an asset – for instance if you give it away, exchange it or sell the rights to it or you get insurance money if it is lost or destroyed. If you do not sell the asset then the market value of the asset at the time of disposal is taken as its value. The date you dispose of an asset is the date that you must use when calculating your profit – not necessarily the date you are paid.

To work out if you have made a gain you must calculate the profit. Take the price for which you sold the asset and then deduct:

❑ the price you paid for the asset or its value at the time it was given to you;
❑ costs incurred in buying and selling – including valuer's/surveyor's fees, auction fees, the cost of legal advice, stamp duty, advertising costs, stockbroking fees (if you only sell part of an asset, such as part of a block of shares, you can only claim a proportion of the costs);
❑ costs of enhancing the value of the asset – restoration, etc;
❑ inflation (see indexing allowance below).

You cannot deduct the interest you paid on a loan that was used to buy the asset.

If you held/owned the asset on **31 March 1982** you can elect to substitute its market value on that date instead of its original purchase price. This is known as *rebasing*. So any appreciation/profit you made before that date will not be taxed. In this case you can substitute this 1982 value for the original price paid. If you are unsure what value to use ask your tax officer. You **cannot** include any expenses incurred before 31 March 1982. Also note that indexation (the allowance for inflation) did not begin until 1982 so no allowance can be made for inflation before that date. See Indexation below.

However, if you elect to rebase **all** your assets, you cannot change your mind. If you have **not** made such an election you can treat each asset differently.

You can also deduct an *indexation allowance* from your profit. This is an allowance for inflation. For example:

Mr C buys land worth £10,000 in 1985
At this time the retail price index was 95.49
Mr C sells the land in 1996 for £17,000
The retail price index is 152.9
The inflation factor increase over that period was (152.9 – 95.49) = 57.41
Divide this by the initial inflation factor of 95.49
57.41 ÷ 95.49 = 0.60
Multiply the inflation or *indexation factor* by the original cost of the asset
0.6 × £10,000 = £6000
This £6000 indexation is deducted from your profits to work out your capital gain.

To make this calculation easier a list of inflation rates is included in the Inland Revenue notes on capital gains.

> **W**arning: you cannot claim to have made a capital loss if that loss was created by deducting the indexation allowance. The inflation factor can only reduce profits, not create losses.

The indexation allowance can also be applied to costs in buying the assets and costs of enhancing the assets.

WHAT IF I HAVE MADE A LOSS?

If you make a *loss* on the sale of an asset you must use this to reduce your Capital Gains Tax bill for 1996 to 1997. But you cannot reduce the gains to less than £6300 – the Capital Gains Tax threshold. Any additional losses can be offset against other income or capital gains in future years, which is known as *carrying them forward*. If your losses reduce your gains to less than £6300 ignore box **8.7** and enter '0' in box **8.8**.

If you want to use up past losses ignore boxes **8.5** to **8.7** and enter '0' in box **8.8**, then fill in box **8.10**.

If you have made a loss on shares in a trading company (that is not quoted on the Stock Exchange) you can offset this loss against your income to **reduce your Income Tax** rather than against your capital gains but only if you subscribed for new shares.

You can claim as a loss anything that was destroyed or no longer has any value (or negligible value) including shares in companies that have gone into liquidation.

You can also claim losses from a business against your Capital Gains Tax. And you can use losses from some rented property but only those classed as furnished holiday lettings (see Land and Property). You do not have to include these losses here, they can also be included in box **13.6** of your main Tax Return.

CHATTELS

Chattels is a legal term that means an 'item of tangible, moveable property'. This will include items of household furniture, paintings, antiques, items of crockery and china, plate and silverware, private cars, lorries, motor cycles and any equipment or machinery that is not permanently fixed to the building.

You only have to pay Capital Gains Tax on these *chattels* if you make a profit of **£6000 per item** and only on the amount over £6000. **Either** calculate the taxable sum by multiplying the full profit above £6000 by $5/3$ (in this calculation you cannot make any deductions for costs or indexation). **Or** you can calculate the *net gain* by taking the total sale proceeds, not just the amount over £6000, and deducting costs as for other assets. After you have done these two calculations you put the **lower** figure in box **8.1**. If you made a loss you can only claim losses assuming you sold the asset for £6000. If you sold the assets for less than £6000, you must assume you received £6000 from the sale.

Warning: You cannot get around the £6000 rule by selling a set of items separately to the same person or group of people. So if you have a set of antique chairs you cannot claim each chair as a separate chattel. For further information ask for Help Sheet IR293.

You do not have to pay Capital Gains Tax if you sell a *wasting asset* – one which had a useful life of less than 50 years when you purchased it. This can even include racehorses and electronic equipment (but not if used in a business).

SPECIAL RULES FOR BUSINESSES

Generally you have to pay Capital Gains Tax on the sale of a self-employed business or a self-employed business asset. But you can claim certain reliefs to reduce this tax bill:

❑ *Roll-over relief*. This allows you to defer gains (delays you being taxed on the profits) made on the sale of business assets **if** replacement assets are bought. You have to make this claim by filling in a form attached to Help Sheet IR290. You must use the old and new assets in the same trade or another trade that you already carry on or start within three years. Only buildings, land, fixed plant and machinery and goodwill can be claimed.

❑ *Business transfer relief.* This defers the gain made when you transfer a business in exchange for shares. This relief is given automatically but you should still make a note on page CG2 and tick column 7.

❑ *Holdover relief.* This enables you to avoid paying tax on a gift by transferring your Capital Gains Tax liability to the person who receives the gift. Assets which qualify include *business assets,* shares or securities in an unquoted trading company (including those quoted on the AIM – the Alternative Investment Market), shares in a *family business* and *agricultural* property.

❑ *Retirement relief.* Despite its name you do **not** have to retire to benefit from this. It applies to those *selling a business* they have run for at least a year or business assets (items of equipment, machinery, buildings, etc). These assets must have been used in the business for at least a year. You can obtain the relief once you are 50 (if disposal or sale of the assets was before 28 November 1995 the qualifying age is 55) or if you are retiring on the grounds of ill-health. You must sell a distinct part of your business, not just a small part of it.

Full tax relief is given on gains up to £250,000 plus half of any further gains between £250,000 and £1,000,000 (a total of £625,000). But you can only claim the maximum if you have owned the asset for long enough. If you have owned the business for one year you can claim 10 per cent of the gain, after five years this rises to 50 per cent and after 10 years to 100 per cent.

If you have run two or more businesses in succession and have only run the last business for less than a year you can still claim retirement relief by adding the past periods of business together. Ask for Help Sheet IR289 for more details on retirement relief.

Tax tip: Husbands and wives are each eligible for the relief so they can each have a maximum of £625,000 of relief. If you acquired the whole of your spouse's business interest you may be able to elect to have retirement relief calculated over the joint period in business.

You can also claim (in box **8.5**) for costs incurred after your business or partnership ceased. These are known as *post-cessation expenses*.

If you are in *partnership* you are responsible for reporting any capital gains arising on the sale of your interests in assets of the partnership. If a new partner joins or one leaves, your share of the assets also changes so you may have made a gain. Ask for Help Sheet IR228.

CAPITAL GAINS AND YOUR HOME

Your main home is exempt from Capital Gains Tax when you sell it. This is known as *private residence relief*. But there are some exceptions, ie if you sold some land, earned money from your home or used your home for running a business.

You only have to fill the Capital Gains Tax page in if you are not entitled to full private residence tax relief.

Your home may still be regarded as your principal private residence even if you have not been living in it because you have been employed outside the UK or have been forced to live elsewhere because of your job (but not if this is for more than four years).

If you buy a home but cannot move into it because you are unable to sell your existing home you can own both homes for up to 12 months without being liable for Capital Gains Tax. In exceptional circumstances, you can ask your tax office for an extension to two years. The same applies when you buy land to build a house on.

If you have more than one home you can only get relief for your main residence and must nominate which this will be within two years. Fixed caravans and houseboats are also entitled to relief as if you lived in a conventional house.

If your property consists of more than one building **and** has grounds larger than one and a quarter acres you may be liable for some Capital Gains Tax. But generally if the additional buildings and land form part of your garden they will be exempt.

If the property has been partially **rented,** then you could be liable for tax on the area let for the period of the letting. If it was only let for a few years, you will only pay tax on the profits made in those years and on the proportion of the home let. So if a fifth of the area of the home was let, you will only pay tax on a fifth of the profit. But if you only have one **lodger** you will still qualify for private residence relief.

If you rent out or let your property the first £40,000 of gains are exempt. So there is no tax to pay.

The final 36 months of ownership of your main home always qualifies as tax exempt (for private residence relief) regardless of whether you let the property out during that time.

> **Tax tip:** If you work from home – either on a *self-employed* basis or as an employee – you will be liable to **capital gains tax** on the proportion of your home used **exclusively** for business. To get round this use a room **almost exclusively** for business. You will still be able to claim for heating, light and your telephone and other expenses. However, you will not be liable for Capital Gains Tax. Ask your tax office for advice.

If you are still unsure about your tax situation, ask for Help Sheet IR282 Private Residence Relief or CGT4 Capital Gains Tax: owner-occupied houses.

CAPITAL GAINS AND MARRIED COUPLES

If you give something to your husband or wife no Capital Gains Tax liability arises on this gift providing you are living together. Remember, if you give an asset away it is normally treated as though you sold it.

However, if the husband or wife then sells this gift he or she will have to pay Capital Gains Tax on profits made from the date the asset was first purchased, not the date the gift was made. Ask for Help Sheet IR281.

If you are no longer living together the transfer or gift may be liable to Capital Gains Tax unless you separated during the 1996 to 1997 tax year. The market value at the time of transfer is used to calculate the gain.

> **Tax tip:** You can avoid or reduce a Capital Gains Tax bill by making the most of the £6300 allowance given to both the husband and wife by jointly owning assets so you can both use up your allowance or by putting assets in the name of the partner who pays the lowest rate of tax.

OTHER RELIEFS

If you have made a gift, disposed of a home you have provided for a dependent relative, sold an asset outside the UK but are unable to transfer the proceeds to the UK or paid Capital Gains Tax in a foreign country, see page CG14 of your Inland Revenue guidance notes for ways you can reduce your tax bill.

Reinvestment relief can also reduce your tax bill. This applies when you use the gain to invest in an unquoted trading company (or another business if you are self-employed or in partnership). You reduce your gain by the amount of the gain you invest. Shares must be in an unquoted trading company (but this can include those quoted on the Alternative Investment Market) and cannot be invested in commodities, futures, shares and securities firms or businesses dealing in land and those providing financial, legal or accountancy services.

FILLING IN YOUR CAPITAL GAINS TAX FORM

Page CG2

It is important that you give as much information as possible so that the tax office does not have to make further enquiries. If there is not enough space, photocopy the form, ask for an additional Capital Gains Tax page or send a covering letter with your Tax Return.

Include details like the address of the building or description of the property you sold, the name of the company in which you held shares, or the address and type of business you sold. In the further information box explain your figures, what reliefs have been claimed, if you have only sold part of the asset, etc.

Column 7 should be ticked if you want to claim relief from Capital Gains Tax. For instance if you want roll-over relief tick this box and explain the type of relief in column 8.

Once you have totalled up the figures on page CG2 they only need to be copied into the boxes on CG1.

10

NON-RESIDENCE

This section needs to be filled in so the Inland Revenue can decide whether or not you should be taxed on your worldwide income or just your UK income. It applies to those from overseas who have come to live in the UK (even on a temporary basis) and those from the UK who are living overseas.

There are major tax advantages to being taxed elsewhere – in a tax haven or country with much lower tax rates than the UK – and so the Inland Revenue keeps a careful watch for abuse of the rules.

There are different tax treatments depending on whether you are not resident, not domiciled and not ordinarily resident in the UK. As such all the questions are about you, your nationality and the amount of time you spend in the UK. No income figures have to be filled in. See pages NR9 to NR13 of your Inland Revenue guidance notes for what is taxable and what is not under each tax status.

Generally, if you earn money overseas you will still be taxed on it in the UK unless you are absent from the UK for an entire tax year. However, if you are in the armed forces or diplomatic service or another Crown employee you will be taxed as if you worked in the UK. However, any extra allowance paid for working abroad is not taxable.

To qualify as a non-resident you must spend **less** than 183 days in the UK in any tax year and less than 91 days a year over a four-year average (for this Tax Return that will be since 5 April 1993). You can be non-resident on a yearly basis – it does not have to be permanent.

The advantage of being a non-resident is that you pay UK Income Tax **only** on your UK earnings and **not** on your worldwide income. But remember you will have to pay tax in the country where you are living.

If you have only recently left the UK (since 6 April 1996) and were ordinarily resident in the UK in the tax year ending 5 April 1996 you **cannot** claim to be a non-resident. Only if you have:

❑ spent the last tax year abroad (you left the UK before 6 April 1996);
❑ are working full-time in another country;
❑ have settled in another country and made it your home; or
❑ are intending to live in that country for another three years;

can you now claim to be **non-resident** provided you meet the rules of spending fewer than 183 days in the UK in any one tax year or visiting the UK for fewer than 91 days over a four-year average.

You will count as non-resident from the day after you leave the UK until the day before you come back to live in the UK.

> **Warning:** The rules covering the number of days you can spend in the UK are strictly enforced. However, if there are exceptional circumstances such as illness the Inland Revenue will take these into account.

The reason why the Tax Return asks for your nationality is that certain long-term UK residents are still regarded as UK residents even if they leave the UK for occasional residence abroad. These include Commonwealth citizens, British citizens and EEA nationals. So you may have to prove that your departure is more than temporary. Also, these non-residents can still continue to claim UK personal tax allowances against any income subject to UK tax (which means some of their income is tax free).

You can be resident in the UK at the same time as being resident in another country. In this case you will have to make sure you are not taxed twice on the same income.

> **Tax tip:** The rules covering residency relate to entire tax years but if you arrive or leave the UK part way through a tax year, you should still be able to claim full personal tax allowances (the amount you can earn before paying tax).

> **Tax tip:** If you are working overseas and are classed as a non-resident but your wife/husband is still resident in the UK, you can transfer any unused married couple's allowance to the UK resident. This means he or she can earn more income before paying tax.

Tax tip: If you work overseas for 365 days or more you can claim the foreign earnings deduction which means all your overseas earnings are free of UK tax. There is a box on your Employment pages for you to claim this. You can still visit the UK but not for more than a sixth (or 62 days) of the 365 days.

Different rules apply to those coming to live in the UK. They will be treated as **resident** in the UK if they either have lived or intend to live here for two years or if they have spent more than 363 days here in the four years ending 5 April 1996.

ORDINARY RESIDENCE

This is a more permanent residence status. To qualify as ordinarily resident in another country you must generally be resident overseas for four years and intend to make your home there. The same tax rules apply as for non-residents.

Those coming to the UK to live will be classed as ordinarily resident if they spend 91 days or more per year on average over four years in the UK.

DOMICILE

This implies even more permanence and can have major tax advantages if you choose to live in a country with much lower tax rates than the UK. Generally you will have to buy a property in your new country, make a will under its law, apply for permanent residence (if not nationality), dispose of your UK residence, close UK bank accounts and open ones in your new country. So you have to take major steps to prove that you are a permanent resident in your new country and show that there is no intention to return to live in the UK. Again, you are allowed to visit the UK for up to 90 days a year.

If you are domiciled outside the UK you should be taxed on your worldwide income at the tax rate in your new country. However, UK earnings will still be taxed in the UK.

If you come to live in the UK you will be required to fill in a domicile questionnaire (DOM1) to ascertain your domicile.

11

THE MAIN TAX RETURN: PAGES 3 TO 8

Now that you have filled in all your supplementary pages you should tick the *Step 2* box on page 2 of your Tax Return. You now need to fill in Questions 10 to 23.

Everyone has to fill in pages 3 to 8 of the main Tax Return.

It is important that you do not tick the *yes* and *no* boxes after each question until you have read through all the notes. For instance, you may not realise that all of your savings and investments are tax free and you do not have to fill in that section after all.

 PAPERWORK REQUIRED

It is essential that you have all the paperwork you need **before** filling in these pages. This will include:

- [ ] bank and building society passbooks or statements;
- [ ] unit trust and investment trust statements;
- [ ] National Savings documents;
- [ ] any other savings and investment literature you have;
- [ ] share dividend tax vouchers;
- [ ] details of any state benefits or pensions you received;
- [ ] life insurance policy payment documents;
- [ ] details of maintenance payments;
- [ ] personal pension plan annual statements;
- [ ] details of any other income you may have received.

You should also have a calculator as some addition and subtraction may be required.

INCOME FROM SAVINGS AND DIVIDENDS

Q10: *Savings and investments?*

Some savings accounts and share dividends are not taxable and as such do **not** have to be listed on your Tax Return.

Although the question says did you 'receive any income', this does not only mean that you actually received the money but that your account was credited with interest or you earned income from your investments. It does not matter whether or not the money you earned was taxed or not. You still have to tick the *yes* box if this income is taxable.

Do not tick the *yes* box if **all** your interest and dividend income is not taxable which means it can be earned tax-free.

What does not have to be included in the income from savings and dividends section

This is non-taxable income from savings and investments and so the following do not have to be included:

❑ Unit or investment trusts if you bought them through a Personal Equity Plan (PEP) and have not invested more than is allowed. However, if you have withdrawn more than £180 interest you will have to declare this.
❑ The first £70 of interest from a National Savings Ordinary Account.
❑ National Savings – only Fixed Interest Savings Certificates, Index-Linked Savings Certificates, Children's Bonus Bonds and any winnings from Premium Bonds.
❑ TESSAs – Tax Exempt Special Savings Accounts. If you have a maturing TESSA and have kept your investment for five years this is tax free.
❑ SAYE – Save-As-You-Earn accounts. These were withdrawn from 1 December 1994 although you can still invest in them to buy shares in the company you work for.
❑ Dividends from ordinary shares in Venture Capital Trusts.

> **Tax tip**: Some £767 million of tax is wasted by unit trust, investment trust and share investors who do not make the most of PEPs – consider these as an investment, particularly if you are a higher rate taxpayer. All income and capital gains are tax free, the minimum investment is low and you can withdraw your money at any time.

> **Warning**: If you put savings into your children's name or into a children's account and the child is under 18 you may have to pay tax. If the interest is above £100 gross (before tax is deducted) a year you will pay tax.

WHAT SHOULD GO ELSEWHERE ON YOUR TAX RETURN

Foreign income

Unless you receive foreign income dividends from UK companies or authorised UK unit and investment trusts.

Capital gains

Profits you make when you sell your investments, shares and life insurance policies (these will be covered on a later page).

If you have been asked to include interest or dividends elsewhere on your Tax Return

For instance, if you are self-employed, in partnership or receiving trust income make sure you only include income here that you have not put on these other pages.

Important note for those with joint accounts and joint investments

If you have a savings account or shares in a joint name, only include your share of the income. This will usually be half.

Tax tip: If one spouse is a higher-rate taxpayer and the other is a non-taxpayer or pays tax at the lower or basic rate, you will save tax by putting all or most of the investment into the name of the partner who pays the least tax. You cannot backdate the way you split income. But if you want to, you should elect to change the way it is split now. Ask your tax office for advice.

Important note for those who receive gross interest (without tax already deducted)

These are accounts that pay interest *gross*, which means no tax is deducted 'at source' by the bank or building society. Remember, just because interest is paid gross does not mean that it is not taxable.

If you opened a savings account that pays interest gross before 6 April 1994 you do not list the interest received in only the 6 April 1996 to 5 April 1997 tax year. You may have to do an additional calculation before filling in your interest figures. This is because gross paying accounts were taxed differently. Last year, the 1995 to 1996 tax year, you were taxed on gross interest paid to you in the 1994/1995 year. From now on, and for any accounts opened on or after 6 April 1994, interest will be taxed at the end of the year in which you earn it not at the end of the year after.

If you have one of these pre 6 April 1994 accounts you must include interest received gross in the 1995 to 1996 tax year and the 1996 to 1997 tax year. Add together the total interest for the two years and then **halve** that figure. This will be the figure you should write in box **10.1.**

Warning: Because you are allowed to halve the tax you pay over the two years 1995 to 1996 and 1996 to 1997 the Inland Revenue will be watching out for those who abuse this. So if you have made any large deposits with a view to reducing your tax liability this will be spotted.

Important note for those with more than one investment

If you have several building society accounts, unit trusts or share investments you must add up the total amount of each type of income before filling in each box.

HOW TO WORK OUT THE GROSS AMOUNT ON TAXED INTEREST AND DIVIDENDS

Gross simply means the amount before tax is deducted. To calculate this figure add together the amount you received after tax and the tax that was deducted. If you have any interest that is already paid gross, this should be totalled up and the amount written in box **10.1.**

> **Tax tip:** Income from savings and share dividends is taxed at 20 per cent. Basic rate taxpayers who pay tax at 24 per cent do **not** have to pay an extra 4 per cent. However, higher rate taxpayers pay the full 40 per cent tax and so must pay an extra 20 per cent tax. Remember, your savings income is **added** to all your other income when your tax rules are worked out. This means that interest and dividends can push you into the higher-rate tax bracket.

WHAT IF I DO NOT HAVE ALL THE PAPERWORK?

Ask your bank or building society to send you a tax deduction certificate. Share dividends should be paid to you with a tax voucher attached. Unit trust and investment trust companies should also give you an annual statement or tax voucher.

> **Tax tip:** If you do not need your investment income because you have other income, consider switching your investments into schemes that give you capital growth rather than income. This is because most or all of the investment will be taxed as a profit under Capital Gains Tax. The allowance for capital gains is far higher than that for Income Tax and many taxpayers fail to use up this allowance.

Q11: STATE PENSIONS AND BENEFITS

See the list in Section 3 of this book to find out which State benefits are taxable (you must pay tax on them) and which are not. You must enter the full amount you were *entitled to* in the tax year from 6 April 1996 to 5 April 1997.

A full list of what should be included in this section is given on page 13 of your Inland Revenue guidance notes. Remember, pensions received from another country must be included on the Foreign pages. If you want these pages ring the Orderline on 0645 000 404.

If you are not sure how much you received ask the Benefit Agency (part of the Department of Social Security) for a statement. You will find the telephone number of your local office in the telephone directory.

You will find the figure for Statutory Sick Pay and Statutory Maternity Pay on your P60 or P45. Maternity Allowance is not taxable.

Tax tip: If you are coming up to retirement and do not need to take your pension you can defer it and take it at a later date. Not only will this increase your pension later on (when you might need the extra money) but you can defer paying tax on the pension until you receive it. So if you have a high income now and will have a much lower income later on, you will be taxed on your State pension or company pension at a lower rate.

If you receive a war widow's pension or are a dependant of a deceased former member of the Forces or Merchant Navy, ask for Help Sheet IR310 from the Orderline on 0645 000 404. This will tell you if you can receive your pension tax free and, if not, how much tax you need to pay.

OTHER PENSIONS AND RETIREMENT ANNUITIES

These include the following UK pensions:

❑ Pensions from your former employer or your late spouse's former employer (company pension schemes).

❑ Income from personal pension plans – including income with-drawals where no annuity has been purchased. An annuity is bought with the proceeds to provide you with an income for life.

❑ Income from FSAVCs – top-up pensions known as Free Standing Additional Voluntary Contributions. But refunds of surplus AVCs should go in boxes **12.10** to **12.12**. These will be refunds because you have paid in more than is allowed as a percentage of your income.

❑ Income from retirement annuity contracts.

Purchased life annuities (lump sum investments that give you an income for the rest of your life) which are not linked to a pension should be included in boxes **11.10** to **11 12**.

If you receive a company pension you should have received it with tax already deducted. You should also get form P60 by 31 May 1997 from your former employer detailing how much tax you have paid.

The exemption/deduction box refers to pensions for wounds, dis-ability and war wounds in military service and pensions paid to those disabled by work injuries or work-related illnesses. Those who worked overseas may also get a reduction in the tax they have to pay. See page 14 of your Tax Return guide.

Q12: TAXABLE MAINTENANCE OR ALIMONY

If you receive *voluntary* maintenance payments or payments under an agreement or *court order* made **on or after 15 March 1988** you do **not** have to pay tax and do not have to include these payments in your Tax Return.

Maintenance payments agreed or made by court order **before 15 March 1988** are taxable. However, if you are separated or divorced from the payer, *the first £1790 of maintenance payments is free of tax.* Anything over this sum is taxable. Payments directly to children or stepchildren are taxable on the full amount. The exempt amount in box **12.2** will either be the £1790 allowance or the amount you received if this is lower.

If you do have to pay tax it will be on the amount you were due to receive in the 6 April 1988 to 5 April 1989 tax year (this is the year when these rules began) regardless of whether you receive higher maintenance now. If you receive less now, you will pay tax on the lower amount.

GAINS ON UK LIFE INSURANCE POLICIES

Do not think you have to fill this in just because your life insurance policy has matured (paid out). Most life insurance policies are **not** taxable.

To be exempt from tax you must have a *qualifying policy*; that is, one which requires you to pay premiums monthly or annually for at least 10 years.

If you cash in a policy before 10 years are up, provided you have been paying regular premiums for at least three-quarters of the term of the policy or 10 years (whichever is less) your gain remains tax free. If you cash in the policy before then, your policy is treated as a non-qualifying policy and you will be taxed. This is why you have to write the number of years you have held the policy on your Tax Return. Note this is the number of *complete years*, not part years.

Non-qualifying policies are those used for investment and are often called investment bonds. These often only require one payment. You will pay tax on the difference between what is paid out (the maturity proceeds) and the amount you paid in premiums. Some of these policies allow you to make 5 per cent withdrawals every year. The life assurance company will give you a 'chargeable event' certificate showing that a potentially taxable withdrawal has been made.

Tax tip: If you are a basic rate taxpayer you do not have to pay tax on non-qualifying life insurance polices, life annuities and capital redemption polices. You only have to pay extra tax if you are a 40 per cent taxpayer.

Tax tip: The proceeds of a taxable life insurance policy or investment bond may push you into the 40 per cent tax bracket. This is because the income you receive is added to your total income and only then is your rate of tax calculated. To get round this you can ask for what is called *top-slicing relief*.

This means that you work out your average yearly gain over the number of years that the policy ran. Only put the average yearly gain figure on your Tax Return. So if you have had the policy for five years, divide the gain by five.

To calculate the tax, multiply the higher-rate tax on the average yearly gain by the number of years you have had the policy. Remember, you only pay tax at the higher rate (40 per cent) – so deduct basic rate tax (24 per cent) when working out this calculation. If you have cashed in part of the policy, you can only average the number of years since the part withdrawal.

HOW TO CALCULATE NOTIONAL TAX

Most life companies will have already paid tax on their profits, capital gains and income from investments. This is the 'notional' tax that you have effectively paid on your life insurance policy. To work it out simply deduct 24 per cent of the amount you receive (the figure in box **12.8**) and write this in the notional tax box. Friendly societies do not have to pay notional tax, so include the full gain in box **12.5**. If you are unsure whether notional tax has been deducted or not ask your investment adviser or the life insurance/investment company.

Box **12.9** will only apply if you have made taxable withdrawals during the term of the policy and these have already been taxed.

SURPLUS ADDITIONAL VOLUNTARY CONTRIBUTIONS

When you pay into a company pension scheme you receive tax relief at your top rate of tax: that is, 40p for every £1 you invest if you are a higher-rate taxpayer. However, this tax-break is restricted. You can only pay 15 per cent of your earnings if you are in a company scheme. If you want to increase your contributions to a company pensions scheme, you can do this by making Additional Voluntary Contributions.

If you have exceeded the 15 per cent limit you will get a certificate from your pension scheme provider showing you the amount of surplus and the amount of tax refunded to you on leaving pensionable employment or retirement. Enter the total amount of the AVC (not the amount you received) in box **12.12**, the amount you actually received as a refund in box **12.10** and the tax deducted in box **12.11**.

Q13: OTHER INCOME

This is a chance for you to include anything you have not been able to include elsewhere. In some cases this may be because you did not know where to include this income and in other cases it will be because you want to use the losses to reduce (offset) the profits or tax on another type of income.

Although casual work is normally classed as employment, if it was a one-off payment you can include it here. Profits from isolated literary or artistic activities could be included under self-employment; if not, include them here. However, if your income counts as a 'trade' you will have to include the figures on the Self-employment, Land and Property or Partnership pages.

Read the list on page 16 of your Inland Revenue notes to check for any items you may have missed and look through your bank statements to see if you have forgotten to include any other items of income.

If you have more than one type of other income you must add up the total amount. An explanation on the Additional information page may save the tax office having to contact you.

You can use *losses* (where the amount you have earned does not cover your expenses) to reduce the tax on the same type of income in either this year or future years. In some cases losses can be used to reduce the tax on other types of income.

Losses included in the other income section can be used to reduce the tax on:

❑ casual earnings;
❑ one-off freelance income (but not regular work);
❑ rare literary earnings (articles or poems being published);
❑ isolated artistic earnings; and
❑ sale of patent rights.

If you want to use losses to reduce the tax on items included in 'other income', ask for form IR325.

Remember you only have to include the amount you make as a profit in box **13.3** – so deduct any expenses that you incurred in earning the income. So if you have incurred costs in your freelance earnings deduct these before filling in the other income box. Expenses must be spent solely to earn the income and cannot be spent on things you intend to keep for a while – these need to be deducted as a capital allowance. Capital allowances are the deductions you can make against tax on the cost of buying business equipment and other business assets (see Chapter 4 on Self-employment). Expenses cannot be deducted from annual payments (payments you receive every year).

Write the total amount of other income you received in box **13.3**, any tax that was deducted in box **13.1**, and the amount paid to you after tax was deducted in box **13.2**. If no tax was deducted leave the tax boxes blank. Help Sheet IR325 has a working sheet you can use to add up the figures if you have more than one type of other income.

If you made losses in past years and did not have enough profits to offset these against (your losses exceeded your profits) and you specified that you wanted to carry or bring forward these losses (use them to reduce profits in a later year) write the figure in box **13.4**.

Write in box **13.5** the amount of these previous years' losses you are offsetting to reduce your profits (and therefore your tax) in 1996 to 1997. If your losses are less than your 1996 to 1997 profits you must use up the whole amount. You cannot set losses against annual payments.

In box **13.6** enter the amount of loss you have not been able to use this year and want to carry forward to offset against profits in future years.

Do not include losses from a discontinued business, called *post cessation losses*: these go in box **15.11**.

However, you must include income you received from a business which no longer exists or in which you are no longer involved (for instance you sold it or stopped being a partner). This is known as *post cessation income*. It can include recovered bad debts and royalties. Again, you can deduct expenses. Put the figure in box **13.3**. See page 17 of your Tax Return guide for more information. Alternatively you can ask for this income to be taxed as if you received it in the year in which the business ceased. In this case tick box **22.5** on page 8 of your Tax Return and enter the amount and the year in the Additional information box.

If the income is purely from a change in the way the profits of a business are calculated you should ask your tax office which expenses you can deduct before filling in box **13.3**.

Interest bearing securities including those you can buy to invest in building societies at an above average fixed rate of interest (these are known as *permanent interest-bearing shares or PIBS*) should be included here. Also include government loan stock (but not gilts) and company loan stock. Only include securities which had an interest payment between 6 April 1996 and 5 April 1997. This applies even when you sold these securities but the next interest due fell in this period. See page 17 of your Inland Revenue guidance notes for more information and Help Sheet IR325.

Cashbacks or *incentive payments* should also be taxed although few realise this. If you receive cash, a car, a holiday or had a personal liability waived (for instance a loan written off) as an incentive to buy something (such as a car) or take out a mortgage, you may be taxed on it. Generally, if the cashback is a one-off payment (you do not receive payments in more than one year) it should escape Income Tax. If you are worried ask the company or person who gave you the incentive.

Permanent health insurance is an insurance that pays out should you be too ill to work. You only have to include insurance policies taken out by your employer and if you contributed to the premiums the amount you paid will *be exempt*. You do not have to include any other benefits for sickness, injury or disability paid under insurance policies.

Q14: TAX RELIEFS

Tax reliefs are explained in Section 3: A beginner's guide to Income Tax. Read that to find out how they are calculated and how they are claimed.

They reduce your tax bill by giving you tax back. You get tax relief at the top rate of tax you pay in most cases although some reliefs, such as MIRAS (mortgage interest tax relief), are restricted to 15 per cent.

Some tax relief is given *at source* which means you get it automatically even if you are a non-taxpayer. However, if you want to – and can – claim higher rate tax relief (for instance on pension contributions) you may have to ask for it.

You can only claim higher-rate tax relief if you pay higher rate (40 per cent) tax and you can only claim tax relief at 40 per cent on the amount of income that is taxed at 40 per cent. So if you only pay 40 per cent tax on £1000 of income, you can only claim 40 per cent tax relief on £1000 of personal pension contributions.

PENSION CONTRIBUTIONS

This does not include company or occupational pension scheme contributions taken directly from your pay (you will have received tax relief automatically). However, this section does cover personal pensions taken out by employees who are not in company pension schemes, schemes to top up your personal or company pension (but not linked to your company pension) known as *free-standing additional voluntary contributions*, and any employee contributions to a company scheme which were not deducted from pay.

You get tax relief at your highest rate on contributions to personal pension plans. So for every £1 you invest you get 40p in tax relief if you are a higher-rate taxpayer. Basic rate tax relief is given automatically. When you retire you can take up to 25 per cent of the pension fund as a tax-free lump sum. The rest must be used to buy an annuity to give you an income for life.

There are limits on the contributions you can pay for each year. You cannot pay more than a set percentage of your *net relevant earnings*. This will be your pay plus bonuses if you are employed minus any expenses or payroll donations to charity. If you are *self-employed* or in *partnership* the net relevant earnings are your taxable business profits (your turnover minus your expenses figure in box **3.89**) or your share of the partnership profits (box **4.19**). There is a second restriction. You can only pay contributions on net relevant earnings up to £82,200 for the April 1996 to April 1997 tax year.

Tables 4.6 and 4.7 give the details of the maximum contribution you can make to a personal pension or retirement annuity plan.

Table 4.6 *How much you can pay into a personal pension (contribution limits as a percentage of net relevant earnings)*

Age on 6 April	Percentage of pay	Maximum contribution
35 or less	17.5	£14,385
36–45	20	£16,440
46–50	25	£20,550
51–55	30	£24,660
56–60	35	£28,770
61 or over	40	£32,880

Table 4.7   *How much you can pay into a retirement annuity plan*
(pre 1 July 1988 personal pension plans)

Age on 6 April	Percentage of pay	Maximum contribution
35 or less	17.5	£14,385
36–45	17.5	£14,385
46–50	17.5	£14,385
51–55	20	£16,440
56–60	22.5	£18,495
61 or over	27.5	£22,605

Tax tip: You can also pay 5 per cent of these contributions into a life insurance policy which pays out on death before 75. You can therefore get tax relief on life insurance contributions.

HOW TAX RELIEF IS GIVEN

If you are self-employed the contributions will reduce the level of your profits which are liable to tax. So if you pay in £10,000 of contributions you will get £4000 of tax relief which in turn will mean that £4000 of your profits are no longer taxed.

If you are an employee with a personal pension plan basic rate tax relief will automatically be given as you only pay premiums net of basic rate tax. So if your premiums are £100 a month, you only pay £76 a month in premiums. Any higher rate tax relief will be calculated using your Tax Return and you will usually get this tax relief in your PAYE Tax Code which means you will pay less tax. If you are an employee investing in a Retirement annuity contract (schemes run before personal pensions were introduced in 1 July 1988) you make gross payments to your pension plan. This means to invest £100 of premiums you must pay £100. You get tax relief at your PAYE Tax Code. Even if you do not want to claim higher rate relief you must still include pension contributions on your Tax Return.

If you have net relevant earnings in any year but do not pay the maximum permitted contributions, the difference between what you pay and what you could have paid is *unused tax relief*. This can be carried forward so you can use up this extra tax relief in future years. You can *carry forward* the unused allowance for the next six tax years.

Tax tip: If you are **not** earning enough to pay 40 per cent tax but think you will in future years, consider carrying forward some or all of your unused relief to a year when you can get tax relief at 40 per cent instead of 24 per cent.

You can also *carry back* pension contributions to get tax relief for a past tax year. You can only carry back premiums to the preceding tax year. But if you had **no** net relevant earnings in that year, you can carry back to the year before that.

Tax tip: If you are a basic rate taxpayer this year but were a 40 per cent taxpayer last year and did not make maximum contributions last year, consider carrying back premiums so you can get tax relief at the higher rate.

If you want to carry back, carry forward or bring back payments, or you have exceeded the allowed percentage limits of your earnings, ask for Help Sheet IR330. Doctors and dentists should ask for leaflet IR1 from the Orderline.

Personal pension plans taken out before 1 July 1988 are called retirement annuity contracts. If you pay into both a retirement annuity contract and a personal pension plan there are special rules. Ask for Help Sheet IR330.

Boxes 14.1, 14.6 and 14.11

Enter the gross amounts (before tax is deducted). For employees the figure in box **14.11** will have to be calculated as tax relief that will have already been given on your personal pension payments. To work out the figure, divide the amount you paid into your plan by 76 and multiply the answer by 100.

Boxes 14.2, 14.7 and 14.12

If you made pension contributions in the 1996 to 1997 tax year but included these payments on a previous Tax Return write in the amount here.

Boxes 14.3, 14.8 and 14.13

These are contributions you want to carry back to earlier years.

Tax tip: If you realise you are going to face a large tax bill for the 1996/1997 tax year, and want to reduce it after the end of the tax year (after 5 April 1997) you can do this by *bringing back* a pension contribution made before you send in your Tax Return. This enables you to reduce your tax bill by increasing your tax relief. Put the figure in boxes **14.4, 14.9** or **14.14**.

Box 14.16

This will not affect many people, only those who exceptionally received earnings from employment that were not taxed at source under PAYE.

Box 14.17

These are top-up pension schemes that are not linked to company pension schemes. You must enter the total amount paid. These too will qualify for tax relief at your top rate of tax. But the total amount paid still must not exceed the overall limits listed in Tables 4.6 and 4.7. If you are an employee you can only pay 15 per cent of your earnings up to £82,200 into all pension plans including your company pension scheme, additional voluntary contribution and free-standing additional voluntary contribution schemes. And if you joined the scheme or it was started on or after 1 June 1989, you can only contribute up to £12,330 for the 1996/1997 tax year (£12,600 for 1997/1998).

Q15: OTHER RELIEFS

Read page 20 of your Tax Return guide, which explains these reliefs and what you can claim.

Mortgage Interest Relief at Source (MIRAS) in box **15.2** rarely has to be claimed as it is given automatically and the tax relief is deducted from your mortgage payments. However, if your mortgage is not covered by the MIRAS or you get a free or low-interest mortgage from your employer you can claim tax relief. Ask for leaflet IR145.

Loans taken out before 6 April 1998 to pay for home improvements or to buy or improve certain second homes can also qualify for tax relief.

Tax tip: Mortgage interest relief is equally split on joint mortgages. But if one partner is a non taxpayer and your mortgage is not in MIRAS you could be wasting this relief. Elect to have the mortgage or bulk of the mortgage tax relief given to the partner who is a taxpayer.

For more information on mortgages not in MIRAS see Help Sheet IR340.

The qualifying loans included in box **15.3** are:

❑ Loans you take out to lend money to or buy shares in a company in which you either own 5 per cent of the share capital or own part of the share capital and are also an employee. These are *close companies* and *employee controlled companies*.

❑ Loans to buy an interest in a trading or professional *partnership* or to buy plant or machinery for that partnership or to provide that partnership with capital **and** only if your interest costs have not been included in the Partnership accounts or on the Partnership pages. These payments are not affected by the transitional rules for 'old partnerships' and you should get tax relief on the full amount of loan interest paid in the two years concerned. Loans for self-employment should already be included on the relevant pages.

❑ Loans to buy life annuities if the loan is secured on your main home and you (or the person who receives the annuity) was over 65 when the loan was made (these are also known as home income plans).

❏ Loans to buy shares in or lend money to a business co-operative.
❏ Loans to buy plant or machinery for use in your work for your employer.

Boxes 15.4, 15.5 and 15.6: Maintenance or alimony payments

These are paid to a spouse or former spouse or child following divorce or under a separation agreement. You do **not** get tax relief on voluntary payments, only on those made under a court order, under a Child Support Agency assessment or under another legally binding order or agreement.

You have an *existing obligation* covered by the 'old rules' if:

❏ you make maintenance or alimony payments under a *court order* made **before 15 March 1988**, or a court order made by 30 June 1988 which was applied for on or before 15 March 1988; or
❏ if you make maintenance payments under a written agreement or deed which was made before 15 March 1988 or submitted to your Inspector of Taxes by 30 June 1988.

Compare the amount of maintenance you paid in the April 1996 to April 1997 tax year with the amount of payments on which you received tax relief in 1988 to 1989. Pick the **smaller** of these two figures. Then deduct the married couple's allowance of £1790. This is the amount that qualifies for tax relief at 15 per cent. Put this in box **15.5**. The figure will either be £1790 or the amount you paid in maintenance, whichever is the lower.

The amount over £1790 qualifies for tax relief at your top rate of tax. If you pay maintenance directly to the child you only get tax relief on the amount of maintenance you paid which qualified for tax relief in 1988 to 1989.

If the court order was made on or after **15 March 1998** 'new rules' apply and you can only get tax relief up to the £1790 limit and this relief is restricted to 15 per cent. Tax relief stops if your ex-husband or ex-wife remarries. You cannot get tax relief for payments made directly to a child.

Tax tip: If your maintenance payments have been increased since **6 April 1989** you have two options. If your payments are still less than the £1790 limit you will get more relief by asking for your maintenance payments to be treated under the new rules. This is because any increases in your maintenance payments are not taken into account under the 'old rules'. However, if your maintenance payments are above £1790 you will be better off under the old rules. You must tell the Inland Revenue (and your former spouse) if you want to elect to switch from the old rules to the new rules.

Boxes 15.7 and 15.8: Venture Capital Trusts and Enterprise Investment Schemes

These offer tax breaks when you invest so they are good ways to reduce your tax bill. However, the risks can be high. Tax relief of 20 per cent is given on investments of up to £100,000. You have to hold a venture capital trust for at least five years. If you have invested in an Enterprise Investment Scheme you must have forms EIS3 and EIS5.

Boxes 15.9 and 15.10: Charitable payments

Charitable covenants are legally binding agreements to pay a certain amount to a charity for more than three years. Gift Aid donations must be at least £250 and made in cash.

In both cases basic tax relief of 24 per cent is given automatically as the charity can recover this from the Inland Revenue. If you are a higher rate (40 per cent) taxpayer your tax relief is 16 per cent (40 per cent - 24 per cent). So on a £1000 donation you will get £160 tax relief.

Q16: ALLOWANCES

Allowances are explained in great detail in Section 3 of this book which you should read to understand how allowances, allowance restrictions and earnings restrictions affect your tax bill. The Inland Revenue Tax Return guide will tell you how to fill these boxes in.

Warning: Some £607 million is wasted by 1.4 million people simply by misuse of their tax free personal allowances according to a survey by IFA Promotion. Make sure you are not one of these by claiming all the allowances due to you.

Tax tip: Now that the married couple's allowance is restricted to 15 per cent tax relief there is no point in switching it to the wife if she is the higher rate taxpayer. However, if the husband is a *non-taxpayer* he should switch (give) all of his allowance to his wife so she can benefit from the 15 per cent tax relief on £1790 of earnings = **£268**. If he does not earn enough to use all the allowances he should also give the unused allowance to his wife. The same applies to the blind person's allowance.

Tax tip: If you are separated or divorced and have a dependent child living with you you can claim an additional personal allowance of £1790. You can claim this even if the child only lives with you for part of the year. If the child lives with both you and your spouse you can split the allowance. However, if you have more than one child you can each claim the full allowance for a different child. The tax saving will be **£268**.

Tax tip: If you marry during the year do not forget to claim your married couple's allowance. You can get a proportion of the allowance if you marry part-way through the tax year. So if you married half-way through the year, you get half the allowance.

Q17: TAX REFUNDS

If you have kept your paperwork in order you should know if you received a tax refund.

Q18: CALCULATING YOUR OWN TAX

Only fill this in if you are planning to calculate your own tax bill. Remember, if you do not want to do the calculation yourself you must return your completed Tax Return by **30 September 1997**.

If you are planning to calculate your own tax bill keep the following in mind:

❑ Even if you calculate your own tax bill the Inland Revenue will input every Tax Return into its computer system. This will mean that your tax calculation will be double checked. If you have made a mistake in calculation you will not be penalised although you may have to pay interest on any outstanding tax.

❑ Do not be intimidated. The calculation sheets look very complicated but providing you follow them step-by-step all the calculations are explained. In most cases you will only have to add or subtract figures. In a few cases you will have to work out percentages.

❑ Do a rough calculation first. You can do this using the figures and explanations in Section 3 of this book. Take your total taxable income, deduct your allowances and then work out how much tax falls into each band of tax. Do not forget that the married couple's allowance is restricted to 15 per cent tax relief.

So if you are married and earn £36,000 a year and get a further £4,000 a year from taxable investments and receive a company car with a cash equivalent (taxable value) of £2,000 and company mobile phone which you use for personal calls (this has a cash equivalent of £200) your tax calculation will be:

Total taxable income		**£40,000**
Basic personal allowance	£3765	
- company car	-£2000	
- mobile phone	-£200	
Total allowances:	= £1565	
Total income on which tax is payable		£40,000
		-£1565
		= **£38,435**

Tax to pay

First £3900 taxed at 20 per cent	£780
Next £3901 to £25,500	
taxed at 24 per cent	+ £5183.76
40 per cent tax on £38,435 -	
£25,501	
= £12,934	+ £5173.60
Total tax to pay	= £11,137.36

Minus the maximum benefit
    from the married couples
    allowance 15 per cent of
    £1790 = £268.50

Final tax figure is £11,137.36 - £268.50   **£10,868.86**

Do not forget to include National Insurance contributions if you are self-employed.

You can then check that your calculations using the Tax Calculation guide are roughly correct.

❑ Fill in the calculation guide in pencil first – to make sure you can correct any mistakes.
❑ Check your Tax Return thoroughly to make sure you have not missed any figures.

Boxes 18.1 and 18.2

These will only apply if you are an employee or in a company pension scheme. The information will be included in your Notice of Coding which explains how your tax code is worked out. See your Tax Code for 1997/1998 for any 1996/1997 tax included in your new Tax Code.

The Tax Calculation Guide will tell you how to fill in the remaining boxes **18.3** to **18.9**.

Q19

You do not need to know if you are due a repayment. This box is here to let the Inland Revenue know that you want a repayment sent to you rather than having it credited against next year's tax or given to you in your PAYE Tax Code.

Q20

This is to check that the Inland Revenue has your correct name, address and National Insurance number.

Q21

This is to help the tax office to contact you with enquiries. If they contact you by phone it will be only to check simple items so do not be intimidated. Boxes **21.3** and **21.4** are to make sure you are claiming the right allowances and will be given the right allowances next year.

Q22

It is essential that you fill this in or else you may pay too much tax or have it collected wrongly.

Box 22.2

This will tell the Inland Revenue that as an employee you do not want the extra tax collected through your PAYE Code. If you do not, you will be sent a tax bill to pay by 31 January 1998. If you do, your Tax Code will be adjusted and tax will be deducted in weekly or monthly instalments depending on how often you are paid. Tax owed up to £1000 can be collected through PAYE.

Box 22.3

You can amend or 'repair' your Tax Return within 12 months of sending it in. If you have any provisional figures simply state which ones these are, why you do not have final figures and when you expect to have them. **Do not delay sending in your Tax Return just because you are missing a few figures – you will be fined if you miss the 31 January 1998 deadline.**

Box 22.5

If you are *self-employed* or in *partnership* and your accounting year ending in the tax year April 1997 to April 1998 ends before you send in your Tax Return and you have made a loss you can claim these losses now to reduce your profits and, therefore, tax for the 1996/1997 tax year. This will save you having to carry back losses when you fill in your next Tax Return.

If you receive income from a business that has now ceased to trade or in which you are no longer involved, you can ask for this income to be taxed in a previous year. Make sure you have included this income on your Tax Return or in box **13.1**, which covers other income. Give details in the Additional information box.

If you are an author or artist and your income varies from year to year ask your tax office for special Help Sheets. You can spread your income over earlier or later years so you are not taxed in one year and then pay no tax for several years. This will even out and reduce the tax you have to pay. Again, fill in the Additional information box.

WHAT EVERYONE SHOULD DO BEFORE SENDING BACK THEIR TAX RETURN

The Additional Information box

Make the most of this box. Read through the completed pages of your Tax Return. If there is anything you want to explain, question or bring to the attention of the Inland Revenue or if you are unsure about whether or not you have filled in a particular box correctly make a note of it here. It may answer any questions your Tax Inspector has and prevent further enquiries by the Inland Revenue. If you need more space, write extra notes on an additional piece of paper and make a note of the fact that you have an addition in this box.

Check you have completed and enclosed all the supplementary pages and then tick the boxes in *Q23*.

Do not forget to sign the Tax Return.

Remember to check your Tax Return carefully as once you have signed it you are legally responsible for its content.

Now photocopy all the pages and additional documents. If the Inland Revenue needs to contact you, you will need to have a record of what you have included on your Tax Return.

And finally... if you are calculating your own tax do not forget to pay your tax bill by 31 January 1998. If you are not, remember you may face a large tax bill in January. This is just after Christmas and a difficult time financially for many. Make sure you have set aside enough cash to pay your tax bill.